# Broken & Building

# Broken & Building
## *Nehemiah*

This inductive Bible study is designed for individual, small group, or classroom use. A leader's guide with full lesson plans and the answers to the Bible study questions is available from Regular Baptist Press. Order RBP0066 online at www.regularbaptistpress.org, e-mail orders@rbpstore.org, call toll-free 1-800-727-4440, or contact your distributor.

REGULAR BAPTIST PRESS
1300 North Meacham Road
Schaumburg, Illinois 60173-4806

## The Doctrinal Basis of Our Curriculum

A more detailed statement with references is available upon request.

- The verbal, plenary inspiration of the Scriptures
- Only one true God
- The Trinity of the Godhead
- The Holy Spirit and His ministry
- The personality of Satan
- The Genesis account of creation
- Original sin and the fall of man
- The virgin birth of Christ
- Salvation through faith in the shed blood of Christ
- The bodily resurrection and priesthood of Christ
- Grace and the new birth
- Justification by faith
- Sanctification of the believer

- The security of the believer
- The church
- The ordinances of the local church: baptism by immersion and the Lord's Supper
- Biblical separation— ecclesiastical and personal
- Obedience to civil government
- The place of Israel
- The pretribulation rapture of the church
- The premillennial return of Christ
- The millennial reign of Christ
- Eternal glory in Heaven for the righteous
- Eternal torment in Hell for the wicked

BROKEN AND BUILDING: BECOMING A SPIRITUAL LEADER, NEHEMIAH
Adult Bible Study Book
Vol. 60, No. 4
© 2012
Regular Baptist Press • Schaumburg, Illinois
www.regularbaptistpress.org • 1-800-727-4440
Printed in U.S.A.
All rights reserved
RBP0069 • ISBN: 978-1-60776-511-0

# Contents

# Preface

What does it take to become a spiritual leader? Is there a course we can take? Is there a degree we can get? Are there certain requirements we need to meet? A checklist to check off?

Nehemiah teaches us that leadership begins not with a course or a degree but with brokenness. He humbly recognized that he fell short of God's standard for His people and confessed his sin to God. That humble act opened the way for Nehemiah to become God's leader in post-exilic Jerusalem.

The book of Nehemiah records God's process of rebuilding the wall and city of Jerusalem through Nehemiah, a rebuilt spiritual leader. Nehemiah's leadership of the Jews through years of struggle and triumph provides an excellent example for us to follow, beginning with his brokenness.

God doesn't want us to offer ourselves to Him as a polished, self-prepared person He could use to do great things. He wants us first of all to come to Him in humility with an honest understanding of who we are and an honest dependence on Him. God is not interested in self-made leaders. He is interested in broken servants ready to be built by Him. God uses the leaders *He* builds as the builders in His work.

All adults are spiritual leaders to some degree by virtue of being an adult. Children, young people, and new believers all look to established believers for leadership. You influence people whether you realize it or not. This study is important for everyone.

Let God use the book of Nehemiah to build you into a godly leader and prepare you for the leadership roles He has for you.

# A Broken Leader

*A spiritual leader shows concern for people and God's name.*

### Nehemiah 1:1–3

**"From the end of the earth will I cry unto thee, when my heart is overwhelmed: lead me to the rock that is higher than I" (Psalm 61:2).**

Someone once said the best way to know if you are a leader is to look behind you. If no one is following you, then you are not a leader. In reality, we all have people who look to us as leaders. And they are following us no matter how we live our lives. So where we are leading those who are following is the question we should consider. If we care for those who follow us, then we will be careful how we live.

## Getting Started

1. Are all adults spiritual leaders? Explain.

2. In what sense are you a spiritual leader?

Every adult believer is a leader to someone. Children look to them as examples as do believers who are less spiritually mature. The tasks God gives us as believers will vary greatly, but He still expects us to conduct our leadership responsibilities with godly care for those we lead.

## Searching the Scriptures

This study begins with a focus on the backdrop to the story in Nehemiah 1:1–3, where we find Nehemiah, a faithful Jew, serving in the court of the king, Artaxerxes, in the Medo-Persian Empire.

The Babylonian/Medo-Persian captivity had originally come upon Judah as a chastisement from God due in part to her violation of the law of the seventh-year Sabbath. God warned that there would be one year of captivity for every year of failure to institute this law.

The Babylonian captivity of Judah was originally presided over by Nebuchadnezzar, who succeeded his father as king of Babylon in 605 BC. When Nebuchadnezzar came to Jerusalem, it appears the Jews submitted to him without a battle (2 Chron. 36:6, 7). Thus began the first of three waves of captivity and destruction which Babylon brought upon Judah as her 70-year Babylonian captivity commenced.

Those taken captive in 605 BC included Daniel and his three friends (Dan. 1). Those taken captive in 597 BC included Ezekiel (2 Kings 24:14–16). The final round of captivity in 586 BC affected Jeremiah who was forced to go to Egypt. The city of Jerusalem and the temple were also destroyed in the third wave of captivity (2 Kings 25:1–21).

Daniel 5 tells the story of the fall of Babylon to the Medes and Persians on Oct. 12, 539 BC. The Medo-Persian Empire then had control of the captive Jewish people. Truly God is in sovereign control of the nations.

### Nehemiah's Family and Place in History

Just as there had been three waves of captivity, so there would be three waves of return. Zerubbabel led the first wave of roughly 50,000 back in 538 BC, upon the decree of Cyrus (Ezra 1:1–4).

The group that returned with Zerubbabel was significant primarily for its ultimate rebuilding of the temple in 516 BC, as prompted by the preaching of Haggai and Zechariah.

Ezra led a much smaller group, 7,000 to 8,000, to return back in 458 BC (Ezra 7:1–10). Despite its size, this group was significant for the spiritual revival that Ezra spurred among the people.

Nehemiah himself led the third wave back from captivity in 445 BC (Neh. 2). While the Bible does not record a great number of Jews returning with Nehemiah, his efforts were most significant for what he accomplished upon his return in the rebuilding of Jerusalem's wall.

Scripture tells us nothing about the man Nehemiah apart from the information given in the book of Nehemiah. Surprisingly, there are no direct references to this great leader in the New Testament.

It must have been difficult for Nehemiah's parents to raise their family in a strange land. Judging by the name they gave him—"the comfort of Jehovah"—and the character traits they instilled in him, it seems evident that they were a godly couple. We know nothing of them except the testimony of their son.

3. Why would the name "Jehovah comforts" be a reminder of the need to show concern for others?

History can rightly be called "His story." God is in control of times, events, and people. Although it seems strange that a Jew served in the court of a Persian king, it was by no means an accident. God had Nehemiah right where He wanted him.

By reporting in Nehemiah 1:1 that Nehemiah lived in the Persian king's winter palace ("Shushan" or "Susa") during the winter months (Chislev: November/December of 446 BC), the author was implying that Nehemiah held a vitally important position in the land of Persia, as he was always needed in close proximity to the king. As the Lord had used Daniel in the preceding century, so He again had a man in a place of authority that He would use for the blessing of His people.

4. Knowing that God controlled key people and events in Bible history, can you safely say that He controls key people and events in your life today? Explain.

5. Why is a belief that God is sovereign such a key conviction for a spiritual leader?

6. Share an example of God's obvious working in your life.

## The Setting

Like Daniel before him, Nehemiah was fixated on Jerusalem and, more specifically, its long-destroyed temple. In verse 2 he showed concern for Jerusalem even though he had never yet physically visited the city. In God's plan, he would be privileged to lead the third return back to Judah's capital in just a few months.

The issues referred to in verse 2 came at the culmination of 92 years worth of activity since Zerubbabel first led a return of captives back to Jerusalem. Many events occurred during this century (as seen from the books of Ezra and Esther) that demonstrated the Lord's use of several of the Persian kings in accomplishing His plan for Judah's return and restoration. Just as the Lord used Babylon as an instrument of chastisement, He would use Persia as an instrument of deliverance.

## Judah and Jerusalem after Captivity

Some commentators believe that Hanani came from Jerusalem on business unrelated to Jerusalem's condition (1:2). The text does not explain the timing or nature of his trip, so we do not know with certainty how he got to Jerusalem or why he came back to see Nehemiah. We can say that this episode shows how Judah's population suffered tragic family separations through this time, and we do know that the condition of Jerusalem was foremost on both of their minds.

Nehemiah expressed his concern for the Holy City, Jerusalem, and for its residents. His pointed questions evidence his character (1:2). He especially showed the qualities of genuine interest and concern for others—all motivated by his zeal for the glory of God to be displayed through His people. Nehemiah could have been proudly content with his noble position in Persia and disinterested in Jerusalem and the needs of those less fortunate. This was not in his character, however.

7. Put yourself in Nehemiah's place. What thoughts and feelings might you have upon learning about the plight of your fellow Jews in Jerusalem while you lived in comfort in Persia?

8. What might happen to the ministry of a spiritual leader who does not have the qualities of genuine interest and concern for others?

9. Why are those qualities important for a leader as he faces difficult circumstances?

## An Afflicted People

Nehemiah's direct questions received direct answers. Hanani wasted no time in pouring out his heart to his brother. He evidently trusted Nehemiah and felt he could be transparent with him.

Hanani did not merely say the Jews back home were afflicted, he reported that they were "in great affliction" (1:3). Nehemiah's kindred wrestled against discouragement and danger. Their enemies hassled them relentlessly with political and military pressure, and their enemies had destroyed their efforts to rebuild Jerusalem. Furthermore, the Jews often strayed from the high and holy purposes God had established for them, causing themselves further pain.

## A Reproached Province

Hanani reported also that the Jews in their homeland were in "reproach," which communicates disgrace (1:3). To be sure, the province of Judah knew the agony of shame by virtue of her own apathy and neglect, but since the Jews boasted of a glorious and faithful God, the Lord's own name suffered reproach. Hanani's comments bring to mind the fact that God's people constantly found it difficult to get their spiritual "act" together. In fact, were it not for the fiery preaching of Haggai (cf. Hag. 1:2–5), they wouldn't have rebuilt the temple by this time.

10. Read Haggai 1:3–15. Summarize Haggai's message to the remnant of Jews living in the land.

11. What was the result of his message?

12. Why is a desire to glorify God such a necessary quality in a spiritual leader?

13. How does that desire help the spiritual leader successfully face seemingly insurmountable circumstances?

## A Broken-down Wall

The message of Hanani had a life-altering effect on Nehemiah. Obviously, this was a very pointed and powerful report that he gave him.

Was Hanani merely rehearsing in verse 3 the story of the destruction of Jerusalem by Babylon 142 years earlier in 586 BC? Obviously not, as Nehemiah would have learned this aspect of Biblical history from childhood. The retelling of it—even with an emphasis on the fact that the walls were still unrepaired—would not have forced Nehemiah into action in the way that he responded here.

What, then, was Hanani referring to? The key is found in a rather difficult section of the book of Ezra (4:6–23). Here Ezra is writing about the situation that occurred about 90 years before his own time during Zerubbabel's leadership, when the people of God were attempting to rebuild the temple for the first time (536 BC).

In the midst of his writing, he draws a parallel to something that happened in his time (which is covered in Ezra 7—10). Thus, the situation he describes in Ezra 4:6–23 is inserted without its historical context to explain the type of opposition that the Jews had faced earlier, in the days of Zerubbabel. When understood correctly, however, Ezra 4:6–23 gives tremendous insight into what the Jews were facing probably just a few months before the unfolding of Nehemiah 1.

In our best attempt to reconstruct the situation, we may infer the following: The people of Judah, influenced by the revivalistic fervor of Ezra's ministry, had used funds sent by King Artaxerxes with Ezra (Ezra 7:17, 18) to begin rebuilding the wall of Jerusalem, even though the Jews had no legal authority to do so. When their enemies, the Samaritans, came to realize this, they wrote a letter to the king Artaxerxes, warning him that a rebuilt city would doubtless be a threat to his power (Ezra 4:12–16).

Artaxerxes sent a letter in reply, forcing the Jews to stop rebuilding until he issued any additional directions (Ezra 4:21). The enemies of the Jews, however, went beyond the intentions of the king's letter and mounted an attack upon the Jews, completely destroying the newly rebuilt walls (Ezra 4:23). The loss likely drained the Jewish settlers of all hope and robbed them of a significant portion of their resources.

It was news of such a devastation as this that moved Nehemiah to tears and prayer for his nation. He certainly encountered "troublous times," as Daniel 9:25 predicted. God's temple and people were left seemingly defenseless.

14. What did the broken walls remind the Jews of?



15. In what way were they a symbol of what needed to happen to Jerusalem's leaders and people? What "walls" in their lives needed to be broken down in order for the rebuilding of the physical walls to begin?



### Fire-ravaged Gates

Six major city gates needed to be repaired (Neh. 1:3). As long as this sad condition persisted, the city would remain completely vulnerable to the enemy.

Nehemiah's glowing leadership strengths would develop in the furnace of testing. His concern for God's people was just the beginning of his leadership journey.

We shall begin to see in the next study what types of drastic action he took, and how he put his personal position and comfort at risk for the sake of serving God by leading his people.

### Making It Personal

16. Name some people who look to you as spiritual leaders.

17. What do your efforts as a spiritual leader say about the level of concern you have for those who look to you for leadership?

18. How do your efforts as a spiritual leader reflect on God's name? Do your actions glorify God? In what ways?

19. What are some ways you could increase your concern for those you are responsible for leading?

20. Whom will you be more faithful in leading?

21. Memorize Psalm 61:2.

# Prayer Changes Things!

*A spiritual leader meets adversity with prayer.*

### Nehemiah 1:4–11

**"And it came to pass, when I heard these words, that I sat down and wept, and mourned certain days, and fasted, and prayed before the God of heaven" (Nehemiah 1:4).**

Wondering where the nearest McDonald's is when you have a Big Mac attack? Wanting to know who to call for an emergency tire change? Or just plain clueless of where you are? Ask your mobile device—an ever present help in time of need that, by the way, won't tell you that you have no business eating a Big Mac. Finding out information is now as easy as ever. All we need to do is verbalize our questions.

As believers we may be tempted to see God as outdated and outmoded. After all, God's answers to our prayers don't appear on our mobile screen in .02 seconds.

## Getting Started

1. What problems can you solve by utilizing your smart phone or other mobile device?

2. In what ways might we be tempted to see our electronic tools as a replacement for prayer?

3. Why can prayer never be replaced by any tools as we face adversities?

Nehemiah turned to prayer when he faced the adversities of his homeland. He trusted God and knew that God responds to the faithful prayers of His people even though the answer is not instantaneous.

## Searching the Scripture

Upon hearing bad news from Jerusalem, Nehemiah was brokenhearted. One can clearly see his love for God's city and for God's people. His weeping displayed strong emotion (Neh. 1:4). His mourning demonstrated compassion and empathy. His fasting required personal sacrifice. But his praying revealed his heart of trust and confidence in God.

### Nehemiah Prayed for Forgiveness

As Nehemiah considered the incredible significance of Hanani's report about the conditions in Jerusalem, whereby newly rebuilt walls had recently been torn down and newly hung gates had been burned, he channeled his concern into prayer to the Lord.

Verse 4 tells us that Nehemiah prayed to His sovereign God and demonstrated spiritual sensitivity. As we will learn from the rest of the book, his normal tendency was to take quick action. Here, he paused in broken dependence upon the Lord.

4. Read Nehemiah 1:4–6. How would you describe Nehemiah's attitude as he began to pray to God?

Nehemiah wept, mourned, fasted, and confessed Israel's sin as well as his own. He performed these actions not to gain God's attention by outward show, but as part of the heartfelt process of a special, undisturbed season of prayer. He knew that he needed God's wisdom, and obviously believed that God would truly answer his prayers (cf. Js. 1:5; 5:16).

In addition to his concern, Nehemiah's prayer indicates the incredible depth of his knowledge of Scripture. It is probable that he was aware of every verse of the Old Testament that had been written up until that time. God had uniquely prepared both his head and his heart for the task ahead. He had a deep, intelligent, Biblically-based concern for the work of God. Add to that his courage and conviction, and we see a man whom God had qualified for a special place of leadership.

Verse 5 introduces an important play on words. The words "keepeth" and "observe" are from the same root word in Hebrew, as is the word "kept" in verse 7. The word could be translated "guard." These verses demonstrate that the people had failed to obey God in spite of His careful guarding of His covenant with them.

The word translated "mercy" in verse 5 relates to God's love to His people displayed in relation to His covenant to them. Nehemiah's entire prayer is based on a deep understanding of the Old Testament as it had been revealed up to this time—both in terms of God's covenants (the basic content and doctrine of Scripture) and His commandments (the very words for which Israel was responsible).

This takes us to the heart of Nehemiah's prayer of confession. He realized that Jerusalem's condition was attributable to Israel's sin. Certainly he knew that not all trials result from sin and that sometimes God uses trials to test or educate His people. God's treatment of Jerusalem, however, was spelled out in the Old Testament law of retribution. God promised to bless His people and land as long as righteousness prevailed. Disobedience would result in chastisement.

5. Read Deuteronomy 28:63–67. Which of the retributions listed in this passage do you find most alarming?

The Hebrew word for "confess" in verse 6 means "to hold out the hand; to reveal." The opposite idea would be to keep to oneself. Nehemiah was openly disclosing before God both Israel's sins and his own. He recognized that God was just and righteous in chastising His people.

Notice that Nehemiah was committed to praying. He was intent on praying on behalf of God's people "day and night."

6. When have you prayed about something "day and night"?

7. What was the outcome of your concerted prayer?

## Nehemiah Confessed Sin

8. Read Nehemiah 1:7. What did Nehemiah confess to God?

Nehemiah confessed that he and the people had "not kept the commandments, nor the statutes, nor the judgments" that God gave to Moses. By making this statement, Nehemiah confessed that Israel had violated all three aspects of the law. By confessing his own sins and the sins of Israel on their behalf, Nehemiah was fulfilling the requirement to "return unto the LORD" (Deut. 30:2).

9. Read Deuteronomy 30:1–3. What requirements did God give His people in this passage?

10. What requirement in Deuteronomy 30:2 shows that God demanded sincere repentance?

Like Daniel (Dan. 9), Nehemiah prayed for the nation according to passages such as 2 Chronicles 7:14, confessing national sins and asking for revival in light of the unconditional covenants God made with Israel. There is no specific practice in the New Testament which corresponds to this today, in our relationship to either the church or the nation in which we live. We may nevertheless learn from Nehemiah's experience and allow his example of fervor and intercession to shape our personal prayer and devotional lives.

## Nehemiah Prayed for Fulfillment Promises

At the outset of Nehemiah's prayer, Nehemiah referred to God as the "Lord God . . . that keepeth covenant" (1:5). Nehemiah focused on the promises of God, and relied on the truth that God always keeps His word.

Nehemiah knew the Law of Moses thoroughly. He knew the passages that taught the retribution principle (Deut. 28:63–67), and he also knew the promises of restoration taught in the same covenant (Deut. 30:1–5). This provided the basis for his petition. He is asking God to honor the promises He made through Moses to restore and bless His people as they return to Him.

11. Read Nehemiah 1:8 and 9. What was Nehemiah communicating about himself when he asked God, Who never forgets, to remember the words He commanded to Moses? Was Nehemiah showing he doubted God or that he was taking God at His word?

As Nehemiah began rehearsing God's words in his prayer, he pleaded with Him to remember the word that He had commanded His servant Moses (Neh. 1:8). Certainly, God does not forget. This was Nehemiah's way of telling God that he was taking Him at His Word. He was basing his appeal on what God had already promised.

## Nehemiah Stood on God's Promise

In verse 10, Nehemiah draws on Deuteronomy 9:29. He is hopeful that, as God has "redeemed" His people, so He will continue to care for them in the midst of their troubles.

Nehemiah stood on the Deuteronomic Covenant. In his prayer he identified the remnant in Jerusalem as God's servants and people—the people to whom God had made His promises (1:10). Nehemiah prayed confidently because he knew God had promised to regather His people if they met His divine conditions. As Nehemiah told God that His conditions were being met, Nehemiah stood on the promises of God. As Nehemiah demonstrated, Biblical praying is based on what God has already promised He would do.

12. When facing adversities, what promises of God could you ask Him to keep as a way of showing that you take Him at His word?

## Nehemiah Prayed for Success and Sought to Help

Accentuating the earnestness of his request, Nehemiah offered himself before the Lord to be a part of the answer.

In verse 11, Nehemiah requested that God would "prosper" him. By using the words your servant, Nehemiah placed himself in the hands of God to be used as God saw fit. From merely a human perspective, he was taking a risk by turning himself over to God. His life at Susa was comfortable. His routine was established. He had vocational security for a lifetime. Yet he saw that his spiritual homeland languished, and he willingly sought a way to help the situation. His prayer for prosperity was not a selfish request for personal success. He sought for success in accomplishing the will of God.

The remainder of the book is the story of what a person may accomplish in the work of God when he or she gives himself or herself completely over to the Lord for His service.

13. Rewrite Nehemiah 1:11 as your own prayer of personal dedication to God.

14. Read Nehemiah 1:11. How might our service for God be different if we prayed with more immediacy?

As you read verse 11 carefully, note the immediacy of Nehemiah's request. He asked God to prosper him "this day." It is easy to put off urgent matters that require great personal sacrifice. Nehemiah was willing to be used at once. This, again, demonstrates the genuineness of his prayer. No wonder Nehemiah would become a great spiritual leader.

Nehemiah further asked God for "mercy in the sight of this man"—that is King Artaxerxes, for he "was the king's cupbearer." As the king's personal cupbearer, Nehemiah was with the king of the Medo-Persian Empire continuously. The cupbearer was in place to shield the king from being poisoned. He was tasked with tasting the king's food and drink before the king partook of it. These two men ate and drank from the very same utensils, day in and day out. We may infer from the context of the next chapter that, in the course of performing his duties, Nehemiah had become a trusted and valuable advisor to the king. Nehemiah would not have been in this position if he were not a man of unquestioned loyalty and integrity.

The mighty King Artaxerxes I had the authority to decree the reconstruction of Jerusalem. But it was against Persian protocol for the cupbearer to make a request before the king. The seriousness of this matter was intensified because earlier this same king had issued a decree ordering a suspension of Jerusalem's reconstruction (see Ezra 4:21).

15. Nehemiah was obviously fearful of the prospect of making a request of the king. What responses could Nehemiah have had instead of praying about the difficult task?

16. What is your typical response when you are faced with a difficult task as you serve God?

It is significant that God sovereignly placed Nehemiah under the only man in the Persian Empire who could reverse his own decree! Nehemiah knew that God moves the hearts of kings (cf. Prov. 21:1). So he prayed for mercy in this king's eyes. Here again is this wonderful balance of divine sovereignty and human responsibility.

We may wonder for how long Nehemiah actually prayed. According to Verse 4, it was for "certain days." Verse 6 says that he prayed "day and night" during this time. But when we turn to chapter 2, we learn that his season of prayer actually lasted roughly four months, until the month of Nisan, or March/April, of 445 BC. What an intense, single-minded burden he had for the work of the Lord!

### Making It Personal

17. Rate your prayer life. Can you honestly say you are a person of prayer? If not, why not?

Spend time with God in adoration, confession, thanksgiving, and supplication on a regular basis. Setting aside a time and a place to pray each day is a good starting point.

18. What adversities are you facing in your life right now?

19. How have you responded to those adversities? Has prayer been one of your responses?

In Philippians 4:6 and 7 God promises to provide peace to those who pray in the midst of adversity. Pray specifically and regularly about the adversities you face.

20. Memorize Nehemiah 1:4.

**Lesson 3**

# Holy Boldness

*A spiritual leader boldly takes appropriate
action because he trusts in God.*

### Nehemiah 2:1–8

**"So that we may boldly say, The Lord is my
helper, and I will not fear what man shall do
unto me" (Hebrews 13:6).**

Fill in the blank: "I don't know how else to say this, but . . ."
("I'm in trouble and need to borrow money," "Your test
results were not good," "Your dog ran away three days ago"). Almost no
one enjoys having these types of conversations. Dreaded important conversations can drive us crazy until we finally get them over with.

Nehemiah faced one of those dreaded conversations, except an
awkward moment was not his biggest fear. He feared for his life. But
God gave Nehemiah boldness, and Nehemiah used that boldness to
obey God.

## Getting Started

1. When have you dreaded having to talk with someone? Perhaps
when you had to ask your future father-in-law for his daughter's hand
in marriage? Or when you had to tell your parents that you wrecked
their car?

2. What motivated you to go through with the conversation?

3. What threatened to keep you from having the talk?

God calls us to obedience and supplies the boldness to follow through no matter what threats we perceive.

## Searching the Scripture

After praying for God's forgiveness and blessing toward the people of Israel, Nehemiah asked God for an opportunity to speak to the king about Jerusalem's plight. Nehemiah 2:1–8 explains how God answered Nehemiah's prayer.

### In God's Time

In the month Chislev (November/December) Nehemiah asked God to prosper him "this day" (Neh. 1:1, 11). However, God answered Nehemiah's request in the month Nisan (March/April; 2:1), four months later.

Often, man's timetable doesn't match that of the all-wise God. God answered Nehemiah's prayer in His good time—and Nehemiah remained faithful until then.

4. Relate incidents in which God answered your prayer according to His timetable rather than yours.

Actually, God may have begun answering Nehemiah's prayer on the day Nehemiah uttered it by cultivating a special rapport between the king and Nehemiah. By the time the events of chapter 2 occurred, the king was evidencing significant respect for and sensitivity toward Nehemiah.

## A Fearful Event

One day, when Nehemiah presented a cup to the king, the king observed that Nehemiah looked sad (2:2). His "countenance" clearly displayed the results of four months of anguished, persistent prayer.

Nehemiah had not previously been noticeably distressed in front of the king (2:1). When the king asked Nehemiah why he looked sad, Nehemiah became afraid. He knew that such behavior was contrary to Persian law and protocol.

Ancient kings were not accustomed to anyone being sad in their sight and did not tolerate it, as it could be a sign of bad news or palace intrigue. For a cupbearer to appear sullen would be most intolerable. By appearing this way before the king, Nehemiah was surely putting his life at risk (cf. Est. 4:2). Nehemiah was under total accountability to the king, who held the power of life and death over him.

Nehemiah's appearance, however, also opened a door of opportunity for him. He knew now that in a matter of moments he would finally have the ability to ask the king to reverse his decree (literally the law of the Medes and Persians) by requesting the rebuilding of Jerusalem. At an earlier time, Artaxerxes had ordered all work on the Jerusalem wall to cease (cf. Ezra 4:21), but now God was bringing four months' worth of prayer to fruition in the life of his servant, and He would be using all of these events for the greater good of His people.

5. Is it all right to be afraid even while trusting God? Explain.

6. Share experiences from your own life in which you were trusting God in a fearful situation while still experiencing the human element of fear.

## Wise Boldness

In order to try to save his life Nehemiah could have denied that he was sad, but he viewed the king's question as an opportunity the Lord opened before him. Taking his life in his hands, he answered the king with boldness couched in wisdom. He courageously told the king that the place of his forefathers' graves was in ruins (2:3).

Nehemiah's response reveals his discretion and sensitivity to the Persian perspective. Persians honored their dead ancestors, and carefully preserved their graves. Nehemiah was striking a note with which King Artaxerxes could relate. Secondly, Nehemiah avoided direct reference to the name of the city, Jerusalem. Any mention of Jerusalem would have charged the setting with political connotations. Nehemiah exercised remarkable prudence. He had apparently researched Artaxerxes' previous statement on this matter.

7. Read Ezra 4:17–22. What reasons did the king originally give for not allowing the rebuilding of the wall of Jerusalem?

8. How does the list of reasons help you appreciate the boldness Nehemiah had when he made his request before the king?

9. How does the list of reasons help you understand the boldness God may call you to at some point in your life?

## God's Control

King Artaxerxes did not punish Nehemiah for his open expression of sorrow. In fact, he did almost the unthinkable; he asked Nehemiah how he could help him (2:4a). God was certainly in control of this situation.

10. Read Nehemiah 2:4. How does Nehemiah demonstrate his dependence on God?

11. How does Nehemiah's immediate response to the king's question help you understand boldness? Is boldness a brave performance a person puts on? Or is it a humble submission to God to follow His leading no matter the circumstances?

One can sense Nehemiah's absolute dependence on God throughout this entire narrative. Before even answering the king's question, Nehemiah once again, "prayed to the God of heaven" (2:4). Depending on God's sovereign leadership, Nehemiah desired wisdom so that his words would be effective. Recognizing the truth that even earthly authority is established by God, Nehemiah made his request accordingly. Once again, God would answer his servant's prayer.

## Nehemiah's Request

Nehemiah referred to himself before the king as his servant (2:5). In so doing, he humbly let the king know that he was aware of his subservient role. A proud man might have touted his own official position, political connections, or service record.

12. Read Matthew 23:12. What principle does this verse teach?

13. From what you already know about the book of Nehemiah, how do you see this principle demonstrated in Nehemiah's life, particularly in his relationship with God?



Nehemiah exhibited great courage in asking the king to send him to rebuild the city of his forefathers. This request was tantamount to Nehemiah's asking for a major leave of absence from his job as the king's personal cupbearer.

Nehemiah may have seen his request as being in harmony with that letter from the king sent to Jerusalem to halt the building of the wall. For the Samaritans who received it had exceeded the king's directives and used the occasion to go "up in haste to Jerusalem unto the Jews, and made them to cease by force and power" (Ezra 4:23). This is when the events transpired that led to the condition described in Neh. 1:3: "the wall of Jerusalem also is broken down, and the gates thereof are burned with fire."

Humanly speaking, Nehemiah's hopes hung on the word "until" in Ezra 4:21: "Give ye now commandment to cause these men to cease, and that this city be not builded, until another commandment shall be given from me." He was hoping for another statement from the king so that the Jews could begin rebuilding the city legitimately and with Artaxerxes's support.

By overstepping the authority that Artaxerxes had given them in Ezra 4:21, the enemies of Israel had actually placed themselves in a precarious position before the king. With his own personal testimony providing credibility, Nehemiah was, in essence, presenting the case that the enemies of Judah were also the enemies of the king, and that the Jews were truly the king's loyal servant and allies.

## The King's Answer

After asking Nehemiah how long the journey to Judah would take and when he would return, the king granted him permission to go (Neh. 2:6). The fact that Nehemiah was quick to give the king his proposed timetable is yet another indication of his thoughtful planning during the intervening four months.

14. How do you think Nehemiah felt as the king gave him permission to return to Judah?


Nehemiah certainly never envisioned that he would actually be gone for 12 years (5:14; 445 to 433 BC)! His trip to Jerusalem would be more than 700 miles and would take at least two months.

Nehemiah demonstrated further boldness and forethought as he made an additional request of the king. Knowing that the Jews had many enemies throughout the regions west of the Euphrates River, he asked for documents of authorization that he could present to the governors of each region (2:7). Such documents would guarantee him safe passage through those tenuous lands.

Sensing the full support of the king, Nehemiah asked for timber from the king's forest that could be used in the construction effort. Again, we see evidence that Nehemiah had put a plan in place in case the king would give him a positive response.

## God's Hand on Nehemiah

15. Read Nehemiah 2:8. Why was Nehemiah so bold in asking the king "for the moon"?


King Artaxerxes granted Nehemiah the additional requests for safe passage and the king's timber (2:8). Although Nehemiah used great patience, wisdom, and boldness, he knew God had graciously blessed him.

Just as God had used Ezra the priest, so he also used Nehemiah the statesman to accomplish work of prophetic significance. Both men were incredibly prepared for the tasks that lay ahead of them (cf. Ezra 7:10). The Lord can still use people who He similarly gifts and prepares for

His work, if such people will only respond to His leading and receive the burden and concern that is necessary to engage in such spiritual endeavors—taking advantage of all opportunities to serve Him.

## Making It Personal

Although God sometimes answers with an immediate yes or no, He sometimes wants us to wait for His perfect timing. We must put the requests into His hands and wait patiently for His perfect timing.

16. What requests, if any, are you waiting for God to answer?

17. What challenges are you facing that make you fearful?

18. There are no excuses for not following God's lead in your life. What are some excuses you might be tempted to use anyway?

When challenges make you fearful, you must determine what you must do and proceed in God's strength and wisdom. You shouldn't let your fears conquer you.

19. Ask God for holy boldness and the ability to exercise it wisely for His glory.

20. Memorize Hebrews 13:6.

# Assessing the Task

*A spiritual leader assesses needs before he begins a task.*

## Nehemiah 2:9–16

**"The thoughts of the diligent tend only to plenteousness; but of every one that is hasty only to want" (Proverbs 21:5).**

Some Ozark mountain engineers decided that under the floor heating would be a nice improvement for their home. Instead of installing a traditional system, the engineers connected wood burning stove boiler pipes to a car radiator nestled between two floor joists. The engineers get kudos for being resourceful, but their grand idea didn't really work. They needed to spend some more time assessing their situation.

## Getting Started

1. When have you torn into a home improvement project without first properly assessing the situation?

2. What happened as a result of your hastiness?

Nehemiah showed good leadership skills by carefully assessing the need to rebuild the walls and gates of Jerusalem. His careful assessment serves as a model for us.

## Searching the Scriptures

A leader sees three things: what ought to be done, what can be done, and how to do it. Having heard the report of his brother, Hanani, Nehemiah knew what had to be done. The walls and gates of Jerusalem needed to be rebuilt! But, two questions remained in Nehemiah's mind: what did he need to do? how could he do it? He would have to go to Jerusalem for himself; he could not manage a task of such magnitude from a distance. He would need to see the situation firsthand so that he could properly assess the task.

Following four months of intense prayer, the king granted Nehemiah's request to return to Jerusalem and undertake this great work.

All the difficult physical tasks lay ahead as did facing the powerful, well-organized enemies that would oppose the rebuilding of the walls. Yet God had provided resources for the humble group that Nehemiah would soon organize. Most importantly, God's hand was on Nehemiah (2:8).

### Nehemiah's Protective Assistance

Because Nehemiah understood that every major task requires careful preparation, he spent the first significant block of his time preparing for the task. During this time, he displayed magnificent foresight. However, preparation demanded courage and faith. It included a long and dangerous journey, an encounter with potential opposition, and the need to provide an objective needs-analysis.

The trip from Persia to Jerusalem was an amazing undertaking in Nehemiah's day. He had to pass through numerous provinces in the Trans-Euphrates region before he ever reached Judah. Even if Nehemiah took the shortest route from Susa to Jerusalem, it would have taken at least two months to make the roughly 800-mile journey. This route would have taken him through Babylon, up the Euphrates River, over to Damascus, southwest through Samaria and then due south into Jerusalem.

## Letters and Military Escort

Having already displayed excellent foresight, Nehemiah requested letters of authorization from King Artaxerxes to show to the governors in the Trans-Euphrates region (cf. 2:7). Moved by God, the king willingly granted the letters. According to verse 9, Nehemiah showed these documents to all the governors along the way. This resulted in his safe passage.

Nehemiah was possibly the only Jew who went to Jerusalem in the third return (445 BC). He did not make this journey alone, however. He reported, "Now the king had sent captains of the army and horsemen with me" (2:9).

Although Nehemiah did not request military protection, he would have customarily received it whenever he traveled on official royal business because he was the king's cupbearer. The travel to Jerusalem, however, was at Nehemiah's request, not the king's. Actually, the king viewed Jerusalem with disdain, but overturned his previous decree to permit the journey. By reporting that the king gave him a military escort, Nehemiah displayed his ongoing recognition of God's goodness.

Notice that Ezra, who returned under very different circumstances at a different time, took a different approach when dealing with the same king (Ezra 8:22, 23).

3. Read Ezra 8:22, 23. Nehemiah's use of human protection and Ezra's rejection of human protection stand in contrast. Was Ezra's faith stronger than Nehemiah's? Explain.

Both Ezra and Nehemiah were men of faith. What the one rejected because of faith, the other accepted as from the Lord. If Nehemiah had rejected all military assistance, he would have travelled alone. While Ezra rejected military aid, he did have thousands of traveling companions.

Furthermore, Nehemiah needed help to transport the materials and travel rations.

## Nehemiah's Potential Adversaries

God's work never goes unopposed, and Nehemiah witnessed that as he neared Jerusalem. Sanballat and Tobiah, part of an important counter-theme in the book of Nehemiah, would pose a major threat to Nehemiah's building project. But Nehemiah already sensed their animosity. He reported the cold reception they gave him as he traveled through their region. Who were these men?

Sanballat was a Horonite, probably from Haran in Mesopotamia. Haran was the center of moon god ("Sin") worship. "Sanballat" was a Babylonian name meaning "the god Sin has given life." Sanballat was identified in history as the governor of Samaria.

Tobiah was an Ammonite and therefore a descendant of Lot's younger daughter. "Tobiah" is a Hebrew name that means "Yahweh is good." Ammon was a region southeast of Samaria, beyond the Jordan River. Ammonites worshiped the false god Moleck. Tobiah was a servant of the King of Persia and was identified in history as the governor of Ammon.

These men were living demonstrations of one of the major teachings of the Bible—one that is applicable in both the Old and New Testaments: Satan will always exert his influence to oppose the work of God, and he subtly but effectively uses those who are open to his insidious methods to advance his cause.

It is an awesome thought to consider that otherwise respectable men may fall to a place where it may be said of them: "It grieved them exceedingly that there was come a man to seek the welfare of the children of Israel" (2:10). The depth of depravity that they experienced should serve as a warning to all. May our grief come only when the work of God is hampered—never when it prospers.

4. Why would Sanballat and Tobiah be so opposed to Nehemiah and the rebuilding of Jerusalem? Consider the fact that their provinces bordered the province of Judah.

5. How could their opposition have affected Nehemiah's assessment of the needs in Jerusalem?

6. How might opposition affect a spiritual leader's assessments of needs today?

## Three Days of Plans and Prayer

It was probably June when Nehemiah finally arrived in Jerusalem. He had first heard about Jerusalem's plight in November/December, and received opportunity in March/April to make his request to the king. If he left Susa in early April and followed the shortest route, he must have arrived at Jerusalem in early June.

Upon arriving in Jerusalem, Nehemiah spent three days quietly observing his surroundings—planning and, doubtless, praying. This procedure was consistent with the process he followed when he had first learned about Jerusalem's crisis (cf. Neh. 1:4). No doubt he spent the greatest part of those three days in prayerful evaluation—listening to the people's conversations, generally looking around the city, and assessing the spiritual atmosphere. During those three days, he told no one why he had come to Jerusalem. He needed a truly objective picture of things, and probably did not want to create any momentum until his plans were well thought-through.

7. Why is concerted prayer so important when a spiritual leader is assessing ministry needs?

8. Why might a spiritual leader skimp on the amount of prayer he puts into assessing needs?

9. What are some consequences of implementing a plan before prayerfully assessing needs?

Nehemiah did not begin his task haphazardly, but rather undertook it with the utmost seriousness in his planning and preparation.

## Careful, Nighttime Inspection

Nehemiah's general view of the walls and gates was not good enough. He needed to make a more careful inspection. If he did that in broad daylight, however, he would arouse suspicion or at least curiosity. That being the case, he planned a nighttime inspection while Jerusalem's population would be asleep. He selected a few trustworthy men to assist him in his nighttime ride around the city wall. He would take only one beast—the one on which he would ride—probably a sure-footed mule. At the established time, Nehemiah began his need-assessing inspection of the walls in the light of the moon.

10. Why was it so important for Nehemiah to wait before telling the people of his plan to rebuild Jerusalem?

11. Nehemiah had particular reasons to keep his plan quiet. Why should spiritual leaders today seek wise counsel as they assess needs and begin to formulate a plan?

As Nehemiah began his nighttime journey around Jerusalem, he exited the old city through valley gate on the west side, near "the dragon well" (Neh. 2:13). Riding slowly as he made his assessment, he proceeded southward along the outside of the wall until he came to the dung gate on the southern tip. The dung gate faced the Hinnom Valley. Here, Nehemiah stopped and carefully observed the ruins.

From the dung gate, he rode northward on the east side of the city until he came to the fountain gate and the king's pool (2:14). Here, piles of ruin and rubble blocked his progress.

Verse 15 is difficult to interpret. Perhaps Nehemiah walked up the Kidron Valley for a short distance on foot and then returned. Or, perhaps he took a different path with his beast up the Kidron Valley and circled the northern sector of the city before returning to "the gate of the valley." Either of these possibilities is plausible, but one fact is clear—Nehemiah positioned himself so that he could see the entire wall in the moonlight (2:15).

12. Reflect on the emotions Nehemiah must have felt as he viewed the broken-down wall and gates. What do you think he felt?

13. What thoughts about God undoubtedly went through his mind as he surveyed the ruins?

14. How might a spiritual leader keep his emotions from allowing him to assess needs correctly?

Nehemiah still needed a little more time to draw conclusions from what he observed and to forge a viable plan. He still did not tell the general public about his inspection of the walls (2:16). Also, he chose not to tell Jerusalem's religious leaders, "the priests;" the political leaders, "the rulers;" or the officials, "the nobles."

15. How does a skillful leader know when it is the appropriate time to launch a new endeavor?

## Making It Personal

16. What tasks for God are you currently responsible for at church, home, school, Bible study group, or elsewhere that require some careful needs-assessment and preparatory evaluation?

17. Analyze the task you want to accomplish by asking yourself assessment questions like the following:

- Exactly what needs to be done?
- How much time will this project require?
- What resources are necessary?
- How much will it cost?
- Where will the necessary funds come from?
- How many others need to be involved?
- How will you enlist them?
- What directives need to be established and followed?

Nehemiah gives us a wonderful example of planning, and he shows us that this process often involves much hard work and requires diligence. Sadly, the work of God is sometimes done with little regard for wise planning.

18. Memorize Proverbs 21:5.

# Encouraged to Work

*A spiritual leader motivates others to serve
the Lord faithfully by encouraging them and
teaching them to trust God.*

### Nehemiah 2:17–20

**"Then answered [Nehemiah] them, and said
unto them, The God of heaven, he will prosper
us; therefore we his servants will arise and
build" (Nehemiah 2:20a).**

But would you do it for a million dollars?" Such a question makes everyone stop and think about the "I would never do that!" statements we utter from time to time. When a million dollars is on the line, it affects our motivations. Most people would do just about anything for a large sum of money. Yet we would all admit that there are some things we would never do, even for a million dollars!

## Getting Started

1. What part do motivators play in your life?

2. Describe a motivator someone used effectively in your life.

Nehemiah motivated the Jews to rise and build the wall of Jerusalem by encouraging them and communicating to them how God's hand was guiding him. People will respond to our leadership endeavors when they know that God is directing the endeavors and ensuring their success.

## Searching the Scriptures

The work of God in Scripture is always connected to building. In our New Testament age, church buildings are important to us, and they serve a tremendously important practical function. However, the most important building program on earth during the church age is entirely spiritual. It is the work of Christ in building His church (cf. Matt. 16:18). The epistles bear this analogy out (1 Cor.3; Eph. 2:19–22).

While the work of God on the earth during this church age is ultimately of a distinctly spiritual nature, in the Old Testament nation of Israel it often took on a very physical nature.

### Nehemiah's Call to Action

The city of Jerusalem was not merely a place of sentimental—or even spiritual—importance. In 2 Chronicles 33:7 we read: "God had said to David and to Solomon his son, In this house, and in Jerusalem, which I have chosen before all the tribes of Israel, will I put my name for ever" (cf. 2 Kings 21:7). As workers rebuilt the city wall, they were not merely doing physical work for spiritual purposes as we might today, but rather they were building a structure that God was going to work through physically to protect His chosen nation of Israel.

We do not know how much time lapsed between the events recorded in verses 16 and 17. More than likely, the event recorded in verse 17 took place the day after Nehemiah's nighttime inspection of the ruined walls. At this point, Nehemiah faced as strong a challenge as he had when he approached the Persian king. He needed to present his plan to all the people and motivate them to rebuild the walls! How would he do it?

### Confronted the Need

Exercising the authority God had given him, Nehemiah addressed the citizens of Jerusalem.

3. Read Nehemiah 2:17a. How did Nehemiah begin his speech?

4. Why do you think he didn't spend a lot of time describing the plight of the city?

5. What would be some good guidelines to follow when communicating a needs assessment to those we lead?

In words similar to those in the report Hanani gave to him (cf. Neh. 1:3), Nehemiah used graphic and stirring terms: "distress," "waste," "burned with fire" (2:17). Without a city wall, Jerusalem and its rebuilt temple were vulnerable. Nehemiah's attitude, however, was not one of self-righteous condemnation. He consistently used the pronouns "we" and "us." In fact, when speaking of the distress of the city, he boldly exclaimed, you see the distress that *we* are in. By being up front with the people and by including himself as one of them, he was already winning the confidence of Jerusalem's population.

## Shared His Vision

Having assessed Jerusalem's need firsthand and having drafted a workable plan, Nehemiah was ready to call the people to action. Presenting a stirring and confident challenge to his audience, he appealed, "Come, and let us build up the wall of Jerusalem." Again, he motivated the nation, also giving them hope by including himself in the challenge.

6. Read Nehemiah 2:17b. What did Nehemiah give as the reason the people needed to build the city wall?

7. Whose reputation was on the line as the city sat in ruins?

Although Nehemiah alluded to Jerusalem's vulnerability, his motive in doing so was to encourage the people to rebuild so "that we be no more a reproach" (2:17). This noble reason for rebuilding would certainly have struck at the nerve of every Jew. Jerusalem was the city of God! It was the mount of God's glory and "the joy of the whole earth" (Psalm 48:1, 2)! For Jerusalem to be in shambles was a disgrace not only to its inhabitants but also to its God. Nehemiah was appealing to the people to honor Jerusalem's testimony to the world.

Notice that Nehemiah again placed his emphasis in 2:17 on the whole group—not himself. His vision was for all the people to work in harmony. It was not a scheme whereby he could advance in standing.

8. Sometimes ministry leaders motivate others to get involved in their ministries so they can make a name for themselves. How successful do their endeavors end up being?

This must have been an amazing scene, as Nehemiah confronted the people with the need and the joint responsibility to rebuild the city for the glory of God—in spite of the enemies that were sure to oppose them. Like a military leader rallying his troops, Nehemiah spoke with a passion and a conviction that were contagious.

9. How does a leader's passion and conviction affect your motivation to serve God?

## Nehemiah's Report

10. Read Nehemiah 2:18. How did Nehemiah stir the people to action?

11. Why did the people find the account of God's hand on Nehemiah's life so motivating?

Nehemiah began his report with a negative reference to Jerusalem's desperate condition. But quickly his report turned positive. First, he assured the Jews that the hand of God was "good upon" him. This testimony provided the basis for believing that the Jews could perform the seemingly overwhelming task of rebuilding Jerusalem's wall.

The words, "the hand of my God which was good upon me," referred to both blessing and direction. Nehemiah's testimony would have reminded the people that God had not forgotten them. He was faithful to His covenant. Nehemiah's arrival was a sign of God's blessing on them.

12. Describe a time when seeing God's clear direction and provision motivated you to take part in a ministry.

After Nehemiah told the Jews about his spiritual authority, he disclosed his earthly authority (2:18). The people no doubt marveled as Nehemiah told them of his royal position, the king's new decree and the king's graciousness in providing Nehemiah with safe passage and the necessary timber.

Nehemiah must have explained the significance of his conversation with Artaxerxes. The "captains of the army and horsemen" (2:9) around him would have been a visual aid of the kind of credibility that Nehemiah brought with him to this post.

While Nehemiah gave an honest report of the blessing of the Lord and his relationship with the king, he did not in any way hold himself above any other Jew in terms of his own individual importance.

Within that context, the people quickly accepted Nehemiah's leadership and bought into his vision. They knew that under Nehemiah's leadership they had everything they needed to accomplish the task of rebuilding, and thus responded in unity, "Let us rise up and build." The statement that follows: "So they strengthened their hands for this good work," may describe the people's immediate preparation to participate in the rebuilding project. However, it may mean they encouraged themselves for the good cause. In either case, Nehemiah was certainly successful in motivating the people by encouraging them.

A foolish leader might have driven the people away at the very start and lost his opportunity to work with them. Nehemiah did not blame the people either for trying to rebuild the wall prematurely (cf. Ezra 4:12) or for presiding over its renewed destruction. Instead, he gave them a fresh start and a new opportunity to rebuild Jerusalem for the glory of God.

As we have seen, Nehemiah placed the emphasis on the group as a whole in his short but rousing speech. Nehemiah's courageous call to rebuild the city transformed them, and his vision became, in essence, their own.

13. What will happen to a leader's effectiveness if he does not take time to communicate his vision to those who will participate in the ministry?

Nehemiah's emphasis was on unity, teamwork, and cooperation—and Nehemiah was the first one to make that emphasis clear and to foster an environment in which such a spirit could flourish. In this and other ways, Nehemiah offered an amazing contrast to the men who had previously attempted to lead the people in Jerusalem (cf. 5:15).

## Nehemiah's Determination

How a leader handles opposition can make or break the spirits of those who follow him. Just after Nehemiah delivered an encouraging motivational speech and the people had responded positively, opposition arose. God used this opposition, however, as an opportunity for the Jews to observe Nehemiah under fire. Nehemiah's wise response to the opposition fortified the people's determination to rise up and build.

A third enemy surfaced in Jerusalem in alliance with Sanballat the Horonite and Tobiah the Ammonite. He was Geshem, the Arabian (2:19). Considering the lands these three enemies of Judah controlled, Judah was surrounded by the opposition.

Geshem was a powerful king of Kedar. He ruled a league of Arabian tribes that controlled Moab, sections of Arabia, Edom, and borders of Egypt. He was in alliance with Sanballat and Tobiah.

14. Read Nehemiah 2:19. What did the trio of enemies do once they heard of Nehemiah's plan?

15. What makes mocking laughter such a powerful attack against leaders?

Verse 19 reports that the three enemies "despised" the Jews and falsely accused Nehemiah. They asked him if he would rebel against the king. Perhaps they wanted to frighten the Jews by suggesting that the king would consider their action treasonous and would therefore halt the project.

16. Read Nehemiah 2:20. What did Nehemiah's answer reveal about where his confidence came from?

Nehemiah's reply, "The God of heaven, he will prosper us" (2:20), both silenced the critics and encouraged the Jews. Not only did Nehemiah use a name for God that was familiar in the Persian Empire, he used a title that strongly asserted the sovereignty of God. Perhaps in the use of this title, Nehemiah was reminding his opposition that God sees the difference between truth and error. In any event, He believed the work could not be thwarted as long as the builders trusted in Him.

Nehemiah's second statement in verse 20 demonstrated his character to both his critics and the Jews. He declared, "We his servants will arise and build." Again he stated his absolute resolve. For Nehemiah, this project was a commitment to serve God.

17. Read Galatians 6:9 and 1 Corinthians 15:58. What reasons do believers have for continuing to serve God in spite of opposition?

By telling the adversaries they had "no portion," Nehemiah reminded them that they were not Jews. They did not share in the rich heritage of Jerusalem. In stating that they had "no right," he meant they had no legal authority over Jerusalem. Artaxerxes had just appointed him the temporary governor of Jerusalem, and so this matter of the city's rebuilding was none of their concern. By saying they had "no memorial," he may have been referring to their different religious system, or he may have been telling them that they would not go down in Judah's own history. If this is the case, Nehemiah frankly told them that they had no past, present, or future ties with Jerusalem.

As in Nehemiah's day, building up the work of today is not easy. We face the forces of overt evil from the outside, and we face apathy and apostasy from within. Sometimes just as the really difficult work begins, interest fades, unity fractures, and coalitions collapse. Sometimes our leaders even fail us. Perhaps they lack the courage, boldness, and wisdom of Nehemiah. Maybe they are ill-equipped for the job—or maybe they desert us altogether. May God help us to learn from, then follow, the example of this man who sacrificed so much to serve the Lord at one of the most critical junctures in the history of the nation of Israel.

## Making It Personal

18. What are some ways you can motivate those you lead?

19. Why is encouraging people a particularly effective means of motivating them?

20. Whom do you need to motivate in his service for the Lord?

21. How can you encourage that person in his service for the Lord?

22. Memorize Nehemiah 2:20a.

# Delegate!

*A spiritual leader delegates tasks to responsible workers.*

### Nehemiah 3

**"So built we the wall; and all the wall was joined together unto the half thereof: for the people had a mind to work" (Nehemiah 4:6).**

What do glory hogs, perfectionists, and control freaks all have in common? They all have a hard time delegating responsibilities to other people. They want to control both the process and the outcome of a particular project or task. If you are one of these types of people, then you completely understand!

Regardless of our natural tendencies, we all must learn to delegate if we want to be effective spiritual leaders.

### Getting Started

1. What is the worst responsibility you have ever had delegated to you?

2. How did you respond to the person who delegated the task to you?

3. What was your attitude like as you completed the task?


Nehemiah organized his workers and delegated work for them to do. He used wisdom in making his delegations and his workers eventually completed their work.

## Searching the Scriptures

Having successfully recruited the people of Jerusalem to rebuild the city's walls, Nehemiah needed to organize the workers and the work. Chapter 3 of Nehemiah explains how he did this. It is important to recognize that this chapter is the very crux of the book of Nehemiah—the 52 days of rebuilding the walls of Jerusalem!

This was an amazing accomplishment for these people. The wall was about 2.5 miles long. And every person who worked on that wall was important to God. He recorded the results of their efforts for us in His inspired Word. There could be no higher praise for them than that.

### Delegation of Work on the Northern Wall

In explaining how he organized the rebuilding effort, Nehemiah began with the northern wall and moved counter-clockwise around the city of Jerusalem. The Sheep Gate and the Fish Gate, with the towers of Meah and Hananeel between them, were located on the northern wall.

Wisely, Nehemiah delegated work according to the interests of the workers—where they would be the most concerned and hence the most productive. This is seen throughout the chapter. When his group could have been overwhelmed with discouragement, Nehemiah got them focused on joining together as a team.

Perhaps the prime example of this concept is listed first. When Eliashib, the high priest, and the other temple priests volunteered to work, Nehemiah gave them the assignment of rebuilding the Sheep Gate (Neh. 3:1). They accepted this assignment seriously as a part of their sacred function, and therefore "sanctified" the Sheep Gate for the Lord.

The Sheep Gate was important because of its proximity to the temple and its relationship to the temple. Sheep were purchased at the Sheep Gate, not only for personal use but also for use as sacrifices on the temple altar. These sacrifices provided ceremonial cleansing for the faithful Jews. The Sheep Gate may also be the same gate known as the Benjamin Gate before the exile (cf. Jer. 20:2; 37:13 and 38:7).

4. Why is it wise to delegate work to believers according to their spiritual interests?

The rebuilding of the wall progressed from gate to gate, and it included the gates themselves. This undertaking required an equal distribution of the work force throughout the city. Nehemiah not only assigned certain people to certain tasks but also placed them where he believed their work would be the most effective (3:2). His master plan demonstrated both an understanding of the project and a familiarity with the people.

Nehemiah's organizational skills are manifested in many subtle details of this chapter. Many times in this chapter we find words like "next unto," or something similar—showing how concerned Nehemiah was that the members of his team fit and worked together, and how he emphasized their cooperation one with another.

5. What does it take for a leader to become familiar with those to whom he delegates work?

The situation in Jerusalem reminds us of the inter-dependent relationship that members of the church body have with one another as they serve together in an attempt to fulfill the mission that God has given to them in their community (cf. 1 Cor. 12:12–26). In both cases, every single member is important. Nehemiah's team could not afford for even one member of the wall-building team to be absent or to let down his or her fellow-workers. Their lives were on the line—as was the security of the entire city.

6. What would have happened to the building project if Nehemiah would have selected only those he thought could do the best job?




Nehemiah's description of the rebuilding effort focuses our attention westward along the northern wall, to the Fish Gate (3:3). The Fish Gate is probably the same as the "Middle Gate" mentioned in Jeremiah 39:3. It was the site of Jerusalem's fish market, where the men of Tyre would sell their fresh catch. Local fishermen used this location as their market as well. It was at this location that Nehemiah's spirit as a leader was tested.

The sons of Hassenaah worked on the gate, while Meremoth, Meshullam, and Zadok worked on the adjoining section of the wall (3:4). Nehemiah observed, however, that the Tekoites worked without the assistance of "their nobles" (3:5). These Tekoites represented large groups of workers from outlying regions of Judah who assisted in the rebuilding of Jerusalem. Notice the mention of workers from Jericho, Gibeon, and Mizpah (3:2, 7).

Here is the first hint of resistance to Nehemiah's leadership from Judah's own ranks. Perhaps these nobles thought they were too important to perform such a menial task.

7. What do those with superiority complexes do to the morale of a group of workers?




8. How would you handle this situation as a leader?

Obviously, since such an effective leader as Nehemiah did not receive everyone's cooperation, none of us can expect to recruit every available person for a Christian service project. Nevertheless, Nehemiah refused to become discouraged. He simply continued to delegate the work to those who were willing to get involved.

The Tekoites who did labor performed double work (3:27). Perhaps they were driven by the shame of their own officials, and no doubt they were inspired by Nehemiah's method of handling the situation.

9. Who ends up losing the most when some workers think they are too privileged to work—those who work or those who don't?




There were also other notable people who, unlike the Tekoite leaders, did choose to get involved. Consider the descriptions of some of the more unlikely candidates for this backbreaking work: goldsmiths, the son of one of the apothecaries, and rulers from Jerusalem, Bethzur, Keilah, and Mizpah.

None should have thought of themselves as too important for this task of rebuilding Jerusalem.

## Delegation of Work on the Western Wall

Nehemiah 3:6–13 describes the rebuilding of the western sections of the wall and the gates there. Both the Old Gate (3:6) and Valley Gate (3:13) were on this wall. Already in Nehemiah's day, a section of Jerusalem was known as the Old City. This Old Gate was probably the Gate to the Old City.

The Old Gate gave Nehemiah the opportunity to involve just about everybody in the work, for it would have been an intriguing operation and an honor to labor at this historic site. Appropriately, Nehemiah enlisted the help of all kinds of people, and he delegated wisely. It was at this inspiring location that he placed workers who had travelled from distant parts of Judah (3:7). He used general labor and skilled craftsmen such as goldsmiths and apothecaries (3:8). Apothecaries were probably perfumers.

He also used high-ranking officials, who must have considered this assignment an honor (3:9–12a). He employed women, too, at this location; verse 12 reports that the daughters of Shallum worked on the wall by the Old Gate.

Overlooking the Tyropoeon Valley on the west side of Jerusalem was the Valley Gate (3:13). This was the first gate Nehemiah rode through on his nighttime inspection of the walls (cf. Neh. 2:9–16).

When Nehemiah delegated this work, he gave specific instructions. He told Hanun and the inhabitants of Zanoah exactly what to do: Repair the doors, locks, bars, and 1,000 cubits of the wall southward. It is characteristic of a good leader to give specific instructions. And a clear job description removes uncertainty, anxiety, and confusion.

10. How would you respond to a leader who says he doesn't have time to come up with precise instructions and clear job descriptions?

11. Describe a time when you wasted time by either not giving clear instructions or not receiving clear instructions.

## Delegation of Work on the Southern Wall

On the southern tip of the old city of Jerusalem stood the Dung Gate (3:14) and the Fountain Gate (3:15). Technically, the Dung Gate stood alone on the Southern Wall and the Fountain Gate stood along the southernmost corner of the eastern wall. They were both considered the southern gates because of their location.

Jerusalem's garbage was carried out of the city through the Dung Gate and tossed into the Hinnom Valley below. Fires were kept burning around the clock to consume the city's refuse. The task of rebuilding the Dung Gate would have been extremely unpleasant. Workers would contend with the smell of burning garbage and the reputation of that gate. An effective leader must assign unpleasant tasks as well as pleasant ones, for every necessary task is important in God's work.

Ironically, not far away from the Dung Gate and pleasantly located was the Fountain Gate. It faced the Kidron Valley, which extended northward from the Hinnom Valley at Jerusalem's southeast corner.

A path through this gate stretched southward to En Rogel, one of just two fresh water sources for the city. It also opened the city to the cool refreshing Pool of the King's Garden. At this site, Nehemiah wanted to do more than just rebuild the Fountain Gate and the wall. He wanted to restore some of the old city's original beauty and splendor. So he assigned workers to restore the pool's walls and the stone stairway that descended into the royal gardens of the Kidron (3:15, 16).

A successful leader is driven to excellence. He is not content doing simply what is required; he motivates people to do the best possible job to the glory of God.

12. How might you respond to a leader who places little emphasis on the quality of your work?

## Delegation of Work on the Eastern Wall

Along the eastern portion of the wall stood the remaining four gates: the Water Gate, Horse Gate, Eastern Gate, and the Miphkad Gate. Evidently these gates didn't need repairs, but the walls connecting them required much work.

The people of Jerusalem passed through the Water Gate on their way to procure water from the Gihon Spring, Jerusalem's second supply of fresh water.

Although there was no need to repair the gate, its walls encompassed a sizable public square that needed to be restored. The challenge of restoring the public square was greater than most of the others, and therefore required highly motivated workers. Nehemiah wisely recruited Baruch, the son of Zabbai, to lead this project. Nehemiah 3:20

reports that he did his work "earnestly."

13. Why must a leader match people to tasks?

14. What could happen to a worker who lacks the earnestness or skills to handle a difficult task?

The Horse Gate stood at the easternmost point of the city facing the Kidron Valley. Biblical scholars believe this gate was used for palace traffic. It was therefore viewed as the royal entrance to the city. This would have made the Horse Gate a central target during military attack.

Demonstrating wise insight, Nehemiah delegated those who lived around this area to work on their own walls—that is, the walls nearest to their homes. By asking them to work on their own defense system, he appealed to their sense of vulnerability, knowing that such motivation would assist them in completing the task at hand. Like Nehemiah, good leaders use the motivation of vested interest.

15. Why do workers with a vested interest in the task provide an advantage for a leader?

Because the Eastern Gate led to the temple area, it was known as the sacred gate. Because of its eastern exposure and proximity to the Horse Gate, Nehemiah continued to delegate the work to those whose houses were nearby.

The so-called Miphkad Gate probably served as either an inspection station for travelers entering Jerusalem, or as a civil garrison for either justice officials or military personnel. This would have been a logical spot for vendors to market their wares. Perhaps for that reason, Nehemiah insightfully used merchants and goldsmiths to rebuild the adjacent walls. This would have been their marketplace (3:32). As a skilled leader, Nehemiah made use of the professional interests of the people.

There are 38 individuals, representing 42 different groups of people, listed in chapter 3. History knows almost nothing of most of these people—including their identities. Yet they are known to God, and their heroic deeds are recounted by Him in this amazing chapter. The focus of this chapter is on these individuals, not just their numbers or the results of their labors that can be quantified.

## Making It Personal

16. Why do people sometimes fail to delegate as leaders? Why might you fail to delegate?

17. What are the consequences of failing to delegate responsibilities?

18. What benefits of delegating should encourage you to do so?

19. Memorize Nehemiah 4:6.

# Facing Opposition

*A spiritual leader handles opposition wisely.*

**Nehemiah 4:1—6:14**

**"Also I said, It is not good that ye do: ought ye not to walk in the fear of our God because of the reproach of the heathen our enemies?" (Nehemiah 5:9).**

H e has a right to criticize, who has a heart to help." So said Abraham Lincoln, the sixteenth president of the United States.

Unfortunately most critics have a heart to hurt. Their criticism and opposition of others comes from a desire to tear people down, especially when those people are finding some success at what they are doing.

Critics are attracted to those who are making progress and enjoying success. They love to find an angle from which to criticize success. That being said, responding appropriately to critics and opposition should become our focus. Doing away with our opposition is impossible!

### Getting Started

1. What are some wrong ways to respond to opposition as we serve God?

2. What are some good ways to respond to opposition as we serve God?

Nehemiah responded to opposition wisely. His example provides some principles for us as believers to follow.

### Searching the Scriptures

Throughout this book we see evidence of a satanic plot to destroy the work of God. As we study, we will gain motivation and wisdom to defeat the enemy today in God's strength.

While it is impossible for a servant of God to avoid opposition, a wise spiritual leader will respond appropriately. Nehemiah 4:1—6:14 describes four waves of opposition that challenged Nehemiah's rebuilding effort. It also tells how Nehemiah handled each one.

### Nehemiah Faced Ridicule

When Sanballat heard about the Jews' progress in rebuilding Jerusalem, he was enraged. As governor of Samaria, he felt threatened both politically and militarily by the prospect of a restructured Jerusalem.

Sanballat expressed his rage in ridicule and mockery (4:1). He abhorred the thought of Jerusalem regaining a place of influence in that realm. This would mean economic distress for Samaria, as the trade routes of the day would go back through the historic capital.

Destructive criticism is normally rooted in anger. Sanballat's ridicule of Nehemiah must have sprung from his own jealousy.

3. What are the natural reactions a person tends to have when someone becomes jealously angry at him?

Sanballat had already accused the Jews of rebelling against Artaxerxes (Neh. 2:19). Now he staged a slightly different attack. He mocked

with a sword by his side. Nehemiah also kept beside him day and night a trumpeter who would sound an alert if necessary (4:18b–20).

8. Read Nehemiah 4:20. What gave Nehemiah and the workers confidence as they labored in a dangerous environment?

Nehemiah balanced trust in God's sovereignty with recognition of human responsibility. He was responsible to develop a comprehensive strategy for the defense of the city that allowed for continuing progress. In the process, he overwhelmed and disheartened the enemy.

Workers labored hard, making use of every moment of daylight (4:21). And everyone slept inside the city, fully clothed and ready for battle (4:22, 23). This would protect both the people and the city. There will always be opposition to progress in the work of God, so a prepared defense is vital to success.

## Nehemiah Faced the Sin of Greed among His People

After conquering external opposition, Nehemiah encountered something much harder to deal with—internal conflict. The Bible often points out the reality that the main hindrance to progress in the work of God is the spiritual condition and actions of His people.

9. Is conflict among believers more difficult to cope with than conflict between believers and unbelievers? Explain.

As chapter 5 begins, Jerusalem suddenly evidenced low morale. Previously the Jewish workers seemed to thrive on the energy that resulted from the enemy's attacks. But now note the contrast from the previous chapter: "The work is great" (4:19) and "There was a great cry of the people and of their wives against their brethren the Jews" (5:1). The people were fighting amongst themselves.

The conflict was so intense that Nehemiah had to suspend building temporarily to deal with the difficulties. The motivation to rebuild the walls was temporarily forgotten under the weight of the circumstances. The work of God always suffers when His people lose their sense of purpose and unity and focus instead on problems of their own making.

10. When have you witnessed the work of a church halting under the weight of internal conflict?


The atmosphere in the city was emotionally charged. Verse 2 gives the reason: Jerusalem's food supply was running low. Apparently failed crops, perhaps due to a lack of attention being given to agricultural efforts, had caused a famine. If that were not bad enough, the city had taken on the responsibility of feeding the workers who had come from all parts of Judah.

11. Nehemiah 5:2–5. How would you describe the Jews' treatment of each other?


Those who had food were selling it for a large profit, taking advantage of the situation. These exorbitant prices drove some Jerusalemites to mortgage their properties (5:3). Others were forced to borrow to pay the heavy taxes to the Persian Empire (5:4). To make matters worse, they had to pay high interest rates to Jewish lenders (5:3, 4). Some Jewish families even had to sell their children into slavery to pay these high costs of living (5:5).

## Nehemiah Responded with Confrontation and Restitution

Nehemiah became angry when he heard the cry of the people and received these reports (5:6).

12. Read Nehemiah 5:7. What words in this verse show that Nehemiah was using self-control in dealing with the Jew's gross mistreatment of each other?

Nehemiah challenged the people to fear God and held every of-
fender accountable (5:7b–10). Nobles had to take an oath that they
would do exactly what Nehemiah had outlined and repay the money
(5:11–13). Nehemiah even gave them an object lesson by shaking out
his clothing, picturing what the Lord would do to those who went back
on their word to correct the situation.

These people here were violating very serious Biblical principles.
Nehemiah wanted the people to consider their testimony before pagans,
who could clearly see that some were putting personal profit ahead of
the work of God.

With candor and pure motive, Nehemiah pointed to his own behavior as a better example to the people (5:14–18). He shared with the
people how he never misused his own office as governor for personal
gain. On the contrary, he sought to use his authority consistently for
the good of others. More than 150 Jews were treated to meals at Nehemiah's own table during those lean days (5:17).

Nehemiah could appropriately ask the people of Jerusalem to do as
he had done. When a person lives according to Biblical principles, he
can exercise valid leadership and confront sin!

Chapter 5 teaches us that the greatest potential for hindering the
work of God is found within God's people themselves. The risk is even
greater when His servants have just come through a period of victory
and find themselves exhausted from strenuous effort.

## Nehemiah Faced Plots against His Life

Having overcome internal strife, the people were now stronger than
ever but faced the hardest part of the job: completing it.

The only task that remained was the placing of the gates. Sanballat,
Tobiah, and Geshem were furious at this progress, and must have been
incredibly frustrated that none of their strategies had succeeded. Still
hoping to thwart the completion of the project, they launched a desperate attack on Nehemiah.

First, Nehemiah's enemies tried to lure him to the plain of Ono, about
20 miles northwest of Jerusalem, for discussions. This set-up would have
taken him away from his work and given them an opportunity to assassi-

nate him. They requested such a meeting on four occasions (6:1, 2, 4–7). Nehemiah understood that it is never possible to compromise with the enemies of God in a manner that would please God.

Next came the most diabolical plot of all. The enemies of God had Sanballat's servant hand Nehemiah an unsealed letter. It alleged that Nehemiah was attempting to establish himself as Judah's king (6:6, 7a). They had the gall to pose as Nehemiah's friends, offering to help him out of the predicament they had created (6:7b).

13. Why should you not be surprised that Nehemiah's enemies used lies and deception to try to halt the completion of Jerusalem's wall?




Finally, they sought to discredit Nehemiah. They enlisted the aid of Shemaiah, a person Nehemiah apparently trusted, to lure him into the temple. Shemaiah was to tell Nehemiah of would-be-assassins in the city and invite him to take shelter in the temple (6:10). If Nehemiah had heeded Shemaiah's advice, he would have violated the law of God, for only priests were authorized to enter the holy place (cf. 6:13). Such an action would discredit Nehemiah in the eyes of both God and men.

The enemies of God never rest. What they cannot accomplish through conflict, they will often attempt to do through compromise or conspiracy. Nehemiah provides an example of how to handle such diversions.

## Nehemiah Responded with Integrity and Firmness

When the enemies tried to lure Nehemiah to the plain of Ono, Nehemiah saw through their scheme. He simply refused to go, and honestly told them the work would suffer without his supervision (6:3).

After receiving the fictitious letter, Nehemiah forthrightly denied any aspirations to be Judah's king, and he rebuked the enemies for forging such a report (6:8). At that point, Nehemiah boldly prayed once again.

14. Read Nehemiah 6:9. What did Nehemiah ask God to do for him as faced personal attacks from his enemies?

Shemaiah counseled Nehemiah to disobey the law (6:10). While his words, at first glance, appeared to be wise, they were completely unbiblical. This alerted Nehemiah to the fact that this was neither a true prophecy nor good advice. Nehemiah understood that the law of God forbade non-priests to enter the temple on penalty of death (cf. Num. 1:51; 3:10; 18:3–7). Nehemiah saw through the deceptive plan to ruin his testimony, and his unquestioned obedience to God's revealed Word saved him from both God's judgment and the enemy's machinations.

15. Why is remaining blameless so important for a leader as he faces opposition?

## Making It Personal

16. How have you responded to opposition as you serve God?

17. Is God pleased with your responses?

18. Have you asked God to strengthen your hands as opposition tries to pull you and move you from God's will? Explain.

19. Memorize Nehemiah 5:9.

# Give God the Glory

*A spiritual leader directs glory to God for tasks successfully completed.*

## Nehemiah 6:15–19

**"And whatsoever ye do, do it heartily, as to the Lord, and not unto men; knowing that of the Lord ye shall receive the reward of the inheritance: for ye serve the Lord Christ" (Colossians 3:23, 24).**

Ever been to England? Perhaps at some point in the future getting there may take less than an hour thanks to a transatlantic tunnel and high speed trains moving around 5000 mile per hour. Lack of money, anywhere from $175 billion to $12 trillion, and engineering limitations are keeping the project from seriously moving forward. But if the tunnel is ever completed, consider the recognition the engineers will get for coming up with a successful plan!

Modern construction projects are astonishing at times, but they all pale in comparison to what God does through people who faithfully serve Him.

## Getting Started

1. What amazing things have you seen God accomplish through people faithfully serving Him?

2. Who got the glory for the accomplishments?


When the Jews finished the walls in just fifty-two days and under Nehemiah's leadership, they created a wow factor. But they directed the wow at God rather than themselves.

God wants to do great things through us too. When He does, we need to make sure He gets the credit even when we want to jump up and down and draw all the attention to ourselves.

## Searching the Scriptures

When Nehemiah faced threats, false accusations, and slander from his enemies, he chose to trust in the Lord rather than acting hastily out of fear. In 6:10–14, Nehemiah actually saved his life by obeying God and remaining in the place of danger rather than following man's wisdom and seeking his own comfort and safety.

Now, under the magnificent leadership of Nehemiah, the city of Jerusalem had finally been restored. Ever since Nebuchadnezzar's Babylonian invasion of August 9, 586 BC, the city's walls and gates had been in a state of ruin. Although the temple had been rebuilt under the supervision of Zerubbabel and rededicated in 516 BC, the city's wall and gates had still been in disrepair. Early efforts to restore the wall had to be abandoned by order of Artaxerxes, due to reports of insurrection.

King Artaxerxes reversed his decree in Nisan of that year, prompted by the explanation and appeal of Nehemiah. He even donated wood for the project from his own forest.

In a record-breaking period of just fifty-two days, Jerusalem's population worked and completed the restoration of the wall. This was, amazingly, more than 90 years after Zerubbabel came to Jerusalem in 538 BC with the first wave of those who desired to return from the land of their captivity. We can only surmise that oftentimes the people had concluded during those days that the city was destined to remain in ruins.

Once again, Nehemiah provided the organizational plan and delegation of forces. The project included 14,000 feet of wall, on all four sides of the city. Six gates received major repairs: the Sheep Gate, Fish

Gate, Old Gate, Valley Gate, Dung Gate, and Fountain Gate. All of this occurred during days of famine and military threat from all of Jerusalem's surrounding regions.

## Builders Completed the Wall

The building project was completed "in the twenty and fifth day of the month Elul"

(Neh. 6:15). Some sources identify this day as the 3rd of September. The implication is striking. If the people finished the project at the end of Israel's summer, the workers must have labored through the hottest months of the year! And they did so, carrying the extra weight of military weapons in some cases. Yet, Nehemiah did not gloat over the success. He did not try in any way to solicit any praise or credit. A spiritual leader does not seek credit for tasks accomplished in the strength of the Lord. His intent of heart is to defer all glory to God. When asked about his accomplishment, Nehemiah merely said in essence, "God did it—not I."

3. Read Galatians 6:14. What does Paul say about boasting in this verse?

4. Why is the cross of Christ a good reminder of the foolishness of boasting about ourselves?

5. What has God done through your life that should cause you to give Him glory?

Nehemiah further reported the fact that this entire rebuilding process took no more than fifty-two working days. Understanding that Jews did not work on the Sabbaths, we realize this feat was accomplished in less than nine weeks. Likely, the military threat had encouraged the people to work as fast as they could; nevertheless, they could not have accomplished their task without God's help.

Nehemiah's words almost seem matter-of-fact as he states, "So the wall was finished" (6:15). Compare this with Nehemiah 4:6. It is almost as though Nehemiah purposely avoided any appearance of self-glory over the accomplishment.

It is a privilege to be able to serve the Lord God with our talents and efforts—and when we do so He uses our service to bring glory to Himself, while causing us to mature in His will and plan.

6. Since believers should give God the glory for the work He does through them, does that mean they should never publically or even privately acknowledge people for their work for the Lord? Explain.

Everyone who saw the results realized that the Lord had provided the authority for the rebuilding of this city. Since the opposition to this project was so great, God would receive all the more glory through its completion. This could only be true, however, as Nehemiah's team abided by God's wisdom, plan, and methods.

7. If we serve God for His glory, we will see good results through our efforts. How do we know if we are serving God for His glory?

## Builders Glorified God

8. Read Nehemiah 6:16a. How did the Jews' enemies react to the completion of the walls?

When the enemies of Jerusalem saw the rebuilt walls, "They were much cast down in their own eyes" (Neh. 6:16). None of their attempts to thwart the work had succeeded. They never dreamed that this task could actually be accomplished.

Furthermore, Jerusalem's enemies knew why they were defeated. They perceived that this work was made possible by God. Like so many today who know they are fighting a losing battle against God and continue to oppose His work, Jerusalem's enemies kept on opposing God's servant, Nehemiah.

Along with the perception that God had blessed His people, Jerusalem's enemies stood in awe of Him. Reluctantly, they also developed some respect for the Jews while their opinions of themselves must have dropped.

9. How will people observing your life know that your work is of the Lord? What will clue them in?

10. What do those who are willing to take on challenging work for the Lord believe about God's abilities?

11. What do they believe about His desires?

## Opposition Persisted

The enemies of God neither give up easily nor show concern about engaging in a fair fight.

12. Evaluate this statement: A great work for the Lord always attracts critics and enemies who try to undermine it.

This section offers a key to understanding much of the opposition that Nehemiah and his builders faced in chapters four through six. It stemmed from two unequal yokes surrounding Tobiah, an Ammonite leader (2:19).

Strange as it may seem, many people in Jerusalem were loyal to Tobiah, an avowed opponent of the work. Tobiah had numerous friends in Jerusalem, and he exchanged many letters with Judah's nobles (6:17).

Tobiah's strong influence is explained by Nehemiah in verse 18: "He was the son in law of Shechaniah the son of Arah," and his daughter-in-law was "the daughter of Meshullam the son of Berechiah." Thus, he was doubly connected to "the nobles of Judah" through these mixed marriages.

Shechaniah and Berechiah would have been in the same generation, as were Tobiah and Meshullam. Somehow these family connections gave Tobiah an introduction to the Judean nobles.

The law of Moses prohibited intermarriage, and here is no doubt one of the reasons for the prohibition. These relationships certainly gave Tobiah a foothold among the people of Jerusalem. These nobles were, doubtless, schemers who were attempting to play the leadership of Nehemiah and Tobiah off of each other, desiring to manipulate circumstances to their advantage. This arrangement compromised Meshullam, who was one of Nehemiah's most dedicated workers (3:4, 30).

We find to our further amazement that "Eliashib the priest…was allied unto Tobiah" (13:4; cf. 13:7). Tobiah's supporters gave Nehemiah many good reports about Tobiah (6:19). They also carried back to Tobiah everything that Nehemiah said about him. This was a most unhealthy "grapevine."

13. What will happen to a leader's work if he tries to track down and silence every unhealthy grapevine?

14. What is a better way to handle unhealthy grapevines?

Looking back, it now becomes clearer how some of the people of Judah would have heard and broadcast the message of discouragement that came from the enemies of Jerusalem in Nehemiah 4:10–12. At least a portion of them were under the influence of Tobiah, and doubtless they were worn down by his negative predictions. We can only infer that some people on Nehemiah's team may have actually been working covertly to spread the message of Tobiah through the ranks. The former would have been an issue of incompetence; the latter a matter of evil.

These people who opposed Nehemiah were foolish on several levels, for if their alliance with Tobiah had succeeded, they would not necessarily have been protected or prosperous as a result. They were, in fact, playing a very dangerous game.

The last few verses of chapter 6 seem so ironic. God had used Nehemiah to bless Jerusalem, yet the people pushed him aside for the sake of Tobiah, an envious leader of lesser character who sent letters to Nehemiah to try to intimidate him (6:19). Nehemiah, however, refused to be intimidated. He continued to keep his focus on the glory of God.

15. Read Galatians 1:10. How did God use the events involving Tobiah to test Nehemiah's motives?

16. Why is it significant that Nehemiah's motives were tested as soon as the walls were completed?

The prophecies of Daniel chapter 9 shed light on the events of Nehemiah. Daniel 9:25 gives some details about the rebuilding of Jerusalem: "The street shall be built again, and the wall, even in troublous times." "Street" refers to the open plaza inside the gates (cf. 2 Chron. 32:6). "Wall" refers specifically to the moat around the wall of the city. Nehemiah truly knew what trouble was, and he faced it here from Tobiah and those who were in league with him. But in spite of all this opposition, the initial work on the wall was finally finished.

In our day, the work of building the church is no less daunting than was the task of rebuilding the wall of Jerusalem in Nehemiah's day. Christ said in Matthew 16:18 that we would face "the gates of hell" in working with Him in this endeavor. May God give us, and make us into, leaders like Nehemiah—full of courage and wisdom—who are up to this task.

## Making It Personal

17. When has someone perceived God's work in your life?


18. How did that person respond?


Give God the glory for what He accomplishes through your life. Simply saying "Praise the Lord" (and meaning it) when someone recognizes your service is an effective way to do that.

19. What difficult tasks might God want you to tackle on His behalf? Perhaps He wants you to start a neighborhood Bible study, witness to a family member, or take a short-term mission trip.


20. What truths about God should cause you to be willing to tackle the tasks?


21. What can you do to build your faith in God's ability to work in and through you to accomplish great things?


22. Memorize Colossians 3:23 and 24.

# Act Wisely!

*A spiritual leader makes wise decisions.*

## Nehemiah 7

**"See then that ye walk circumspectly, not as fools, but as wise, redeeming the time, because the days are evil. Wherefore be ye not unwise, but understanding what the will of the Lord is"** (Ephesians 5:15–17).

Decisions, decisions, decisions!" For some people, that is a cry of frustration. Such people don't like making decisions. Decisions stress them out. For other people, it is a statement of anticipation. They love having the power to make all the decisions.

Personality has a lot to do with determining how we view decisions. But no matter our outlook or personality, decisions are part of our lives and part of being a leader.

### Getting Started

1. Do you like being the decision maker of a particular group? Why?

2. Why does wanting to make all the decisions not necessarily make a person a good decision maker?

Nehemiah was God's decision maker in the newly walled Jerusalem. His decisions were wise and indicators of his close relationship with God.

## Searching the Scriptures

Nehemiah didn't pack up and return to Susa when the wall and gates were finished. He knew that there was still much to do. Jerusalem needed its own strong, local leadership. It needed an adequate plan of protection to maximize the use of the rebuilt wall. It needed to be re-populated with some of the people still living in other parts of Judah. It needed an equitable distribution of population. As a wise leader, Nehemiah looked beyond the immediate task to the process of follow-up.

The focus of chapter 7 is on the people who would literally fill the rebuilt city—both for their own protection and also to reinforce it against its enemies.

## Nehemiah Wisely Appointed New Leaders

Now that the walls were rebuilt, the people of Jerusalem needed to post some guards. Nehemiah used his authority well. He appointed "porters" or gatekeepers to stand watch at the temple entrances and at the newly restored gates around the city wall (7:1). He also appointed singers and Levites. Perhaps these singers and Levites were supposed to assist the security force. On the other hand, Nehemiah may have appointed them to reinstitute a refurbished program of public worship. Singers did lead the daily worship services, and Levites functioned primarily as teachers of the law of God. Even if they simply assisted in the watch around the city, their constant presence would have reminded the people to worship God.

Nehemiah also recognized the need to appoint local leadership for Jerusalem. Perhaps the day-to-day details of city management were growing too large for him to handle by himself. In any event, the day would come when he would return to Susa. To leave the city well intact, it had to be self-governing.

3. How can your church's leaders build a strong leadership base for the church's future needs?

## Hanani Appointed

Notice that Nehemiah's focus was on appointing godly, qualified leadership (7:2). The first man Nehemiah appointed to help govern Jerusalem was Hanani, Nehemiah's brother (cf. 1:2). This decision may appear to have been unwise. Nehemiah risked being accused of nepotism—of establishing a family power-base. On the other hand, this selection showed much wisdom. Hanani and Nehemiah shared the same upbringing, training, ideals, values, and commitments. Hanani would certainly remain loyal to Nehemiah and resist the overtures of Tobiah's followers. Furthermore, Hanani had already proven himself as a loyal son of Judah. In fact, back in Persia he had given Nehemiah the initial report of Jerusalem's sad state. He was obviously a man the people could trust.

4. What do you think about appointing unfaithful, spiritually floundering people to leadership positions in order to challenge them to become strong, godly leaders?

5. What potential problems might come from such a decision?

## Hananiah Appointed

Probably because Hanani was Nehemiah's brother, Nehemiah appointed a second ruler—Hananiah (7:2). This appointment would have put to rest any fears of nepotism, plus it added the benefit of additional manpower to handle all of the details of city management. Hananiah was an experienced leader; he had already been serving as the "ruler of the palace." He impressed Nehemiah, however, for more reasons than just his experience.

6. Read Nehemiah 7:2. What qualities made Hananiah a good candidate for a leadership position?

7. Why would a fear of God be particularly important for Hananiah as he dealt with enemies both inside and outside Jerusalem?

Nehemiah considered him a "faithful man" who "feared God." These are two essential characteristics of any spiritual leader.

8. Read Acts 6:1–7. What criteria were used to select the leaders in Acts 6?

9. How do these criteria compare with those Nehemiah used in appointing Hanani and Hananiah?

Hananiah did not know that Nehemiah was observing him as he faithfully fulfilled his daily tasks. Yet, because of his faithfulness, he became a co-ruler over all Jerusalem. When we are faithful in small tasks, God often increases our responsibilities and sphere of influence.

## Nehemiah Wisely Counseled New Guards

Now that Hanani and Hananiah were in charge, Nehemiah gave them some specific instructions for supervising the newly-assigned gatekeepers and city guards. He knew that gates and walls alone could not keep out the enemy. The city needed to adopt a wise defensive strategy as well.

Newly appointed gatekeepers were to open the city gates for just a few hours each day (7:3). Jerusalem, though rebuilt, was sparsely populated (7:4). Workers from other regions of Judah had gone home. It would certainly be easy for unwanted individuals to make their way undetected into the city. Nehemiah planned for the city gates to be open only during the busy mid-day hours, when most of Jerusalem's populace would be out and about.

Also, newly appointed city guards were to keep watch around their own neighborhoods. This was no doubt to be done both night and day. Not only was Nehemiah wise to devise this plan in providing protection, he was wise to use man's natural instinct to protect his own home.

10. Read Nehemiah 7:3. Was Nehemiah showing a lack of faith in God with the cautious instructions he gave to the gatekeepers and guards? Explain.

11. Read Proverbs 22:3. What principle in this verse helps explain why Nehemiah thought it was necessary to appoint gatekeepers and guards?

## Nehemiah Wisely Strategized a New Population

According to verse 4, Jerusalem's population was sparse following the rebuilding project. The city was still being developed, which would explain this situation to some extent. Many people who did not live in the city permanently would also come inside its protective walls when necessary.

From verse 4 through the rest of the chapter, we see Nehemiah following God's leading in implementing a plan to populate the city with those who were of pure Jewish ancestry and who had proved that they were loyal citizens and not likely to be potential Samaritan spies. It was vital that the city-dwellers remained pure and devoted to God, for He was the defense for the city, and the city was the stronghold and fortress for the nation.

The land area of the city itself was quite large. In fact, some scholars estimate that Jerusalem covered about 260 acres. Of the roughly 52,000 Jews who had returned to Judah under Zerubbabel and Ezra, few decided to settle in Jerusalem, probably because they felt defenseless without a wall. Thus, for several generations the Jews had avoided building homes in Jerusalem.

## Clans and Communities

Ninety years before Nehemiah's return, Zerubbabel had taken a census of the initial returnees (Ezra 2). By using this list as a working document for his repopulation plan, Nehemiah provided some much-needed continuity for Jerusalem's past, present, and future. This directory listed some by clans, some according to their original communities, and others by profession or vocation. Those listed according to clan included the descendents of Parosh and seventeen other families (7:8–25). Those listed according to community included the men of Bethlehem and twelve other communities (7:26–38).

Ezra's genealogical record would assist Nehemiah in giving Jerusalem a purely Jewish population. In doing this, Nehemiah would preserve the purity of the nation and keep the lineage intact for the coming of Messiah. Anyone who sought Jerusalem's harm would also be sifted out by Nehemiah's process.

Nehemiah's plan certainly demonstrated practical administrative wisdom as well, for this registration would give him an equitable way to distribute the repopulation.

## Professionals and Vocationalists

The following lists were given in the registry according to occupation: the priests (7:39–42), the Levites (7:43), the singers (7:44), the gatekeepers (7:45), the temple servants (7:46–56), the descendents of Solomon's servants (7:57–61), the descendents of Delaiah, Tobiah, and Nekoda (7:61, 62), and the non-documented priests (7:63–65).

The non-documented priests were unable to prove their ancestry. This posed a significant problem because the law of Moses insisted that a priest must be of the Levitical-Aaronic line. While it is true that some of these non-documented priests may have been qualified, it is also true that some (or perhaps even all) may not have been. It would have been presumptuous to expect God to bless leaders who failed to meet His requirements. Something had to be done.

12. What would be the wise, though not necessarily nice, decision to make in regard to the undocumented priests?

13. Why can't a leader let his decisions be dictated by what would be the nice thing to do?

If all of the non-documented priests had been automatically barred from their temple service, possibly some qualified priests would have lost their rightful ministry. For that reason, they were temporarily suspended "as polluted, put from the priesthood" (7:64; cf. Ezra 2:62). This suspension was temporary until the Urim and Thummim could be consulted (7:65; cf. Ezra 2:63). Through the Urim and Thummim, God would reveal which priests were clean and which priests were not.

Nehemiah included all of these details in his use of the registry. Perhaps he wanted to be reminded of the need for purity among God's leaders. Further, he certainly wanted to remind the people of his day that spiritual leaders must meet God's specified qualifications.

14. Creativity, vision, and a forward-thinking outlook are important qualities to look for in potential leaders. But why should those types of qualities not be the only criteria for appointing spiritual leaders?

After listing the returnees according to these various groupings, Nehemiah gave the totals in Nehemiah 7:66–69. Nehemiah probably took careful note of the final comments made in this registry, for he again decided to include them in his document. After an account of the people's generous giving (7:70–72), the text states that those who knew their ancestral towns settled in those towns (7:73). This information would later factor into Nehemiah's own plan for the repopulation of Jerusalem.

The last statement of verse 73 locks the timing of this episode in at "the seventh month." This is Tishri (September/October). We will learn the importance of that in the next lesson. It is also important to note that this incident took place very shortly after the work on the wall was finished. That occurred on "the twenty and fifth *day* of *the month* Elul" (Elul being the sixth month [August/September]).

The chapter ends with all the people organized under Nehemiah's godly leadership. His model reminds us of the need to stay with a job until the end—including dealing with all the details and every person who needs our help. Chapter 8 goes on to explore the exciting story of the renewal that took place within the rebuilt city. But the inspired author did not rush ahead to the account of those wonderful experiences without first completing the record of all that it took to consider the wall project complete and the city safe.

In summary, Nehemiah followed problem-solving steps in making wise decisions. First he **determined the problem** when he recognized the ongoing vulnerability of Jerusalem. Second he **developed foresight** when he envisioned a future military invasion. Third, his appointments of Hanani and Hananiah as leaders showed that he **drew on others' wisdom**. Fourth, he **delegated resources** when he recommended helpers to Hanani and Hananiah and checked Jerusalem's documents. Fifth, he **drafted a solution** when he devised a plan for a defense system and repopulation. And last, simply **did the plan** by making appointments, giving instructions, and laying groundwork.

## Making It Personal

15. Think through problems you are facing and apply the problem-solving steps (in bold above) that Nehemiah employed.



16. Ask for God's help and direction concerning the specific problems you are facing.

17. Memorize Ephesians 5:15–17.

# God's Word Is Powerful

*A spiritual leader shares God's Word with confidence.*

## Nehemiah 8

**"For the word of God is quick, and powerful, and sharper than any twoedged sword, piercing even to the dividing asunder of soul and spirit, and of the joints and marrow, and is a discerner of the thoughts and intents of the heart" (Hebrews 4:12).**

Martin-Seymour Smith wrote a book called *The 100 Most Influential Books Ever Written*. In that book he listed what he thought were the top 100 most influential books. Not surprisingly, the Old Testament and the New Testament both made his list. Some of the other books on his list were religious in nature. Those books included the Hindu scriptures called *Upanishads*, the Muslim *Quran*, and the Judaic mysticism religious writings called *Kabbalah*.

If Smith's list were narrowed down to the books that are "alive", only the Old and New Testaments would make the list!

## Getting Started

1. In what way is the Bible "alive"?

2. Describe a time when the Bible came "alive" to you.

3. How did you respond?

Though the Bible is alive, that does not mean that all we need to do is read it. We should be committed to studying it and meditating on it so we truly understand it and so God can use it to change our lives.

Ezra took time to explain the Scriptures as he read them to the Jews. As a result the people understood the Scriptures and responded to them.

## Searching the Scriptures

Although the Jews had rebuilt the wall of Jerusalem and had reestablished the community, something was missing. The people needed a renewed submission to God's Word. As a sensitive leader, Nehemiah sought to meet this need and thus remained in Jerusalem. He knew that he must set the example for his people as their chief civilian administrator.

It was now Tishri, the seventh month (September/October) and the most sacred month of the Jewish year. Tishri included three special celebrations: the Feast of Trumpets, the Day of Atonement, and the Feast of Tabernacles or Booths.

According to Nehemiah 8:2, the people gathered at the Water Gate "upon the first day of the seventh month," the Jewish celebration of the Feast of Trumpets. It marked the beginning of Israel's civil new year. What a splendid way this was for Jerusalem to usher in a new year!

### Nehemiah Supported Hearing God's Word

A large assembly ("all the people") had gathered at the Water Gate to ask Ezra to read for them from "the book of the law of Moses" (8:1). They recognized the book as a record of God's commands to them.

4. Read Nehemiah 8:1, 2 and Psalm 1:2, 3. How did the people of Israel reflect the theme of Psalm 1:2 and 3?

5. When was the last time you were hungry to know God's Word?

As Bible-believing Christians, the basis of our faith is the written Word of God, and it is only by that Word that we can increase our faith (cf. Rom. 10:17). Thus, the preferred method of preaching is to teach the Bible "precept upon precept, precept upon precept; line upon line, line upon line" (Isa. 28:13; cf. 2 Tim. 4:2). Today we refer to this as expositional preaching and teaching. Though this term is not used in Nehemiah 8, the concept is certainly modeled by Ezra.

These people were in need of a time of focus on God. They had labored to the point of exhaustion in their efforts; providentially, it was time for rejuvenation.

The completion of the wall was obviously a work of God through His willing servants. His enabling caught the attention of the people and they wanted to know Him better.

6. When God works in obvious ways in your life, how does that affect your desire to know Him and live by His ways?

The section of wall around the Water Gate enclosed a sizeable public square. The crowd had gathered at the Water Gate and included women and children as well as men (8:2). People of both genders and all ages were hungry for God's Word.

Nehemiah realized that "the book of the law of Moses" was not merely the words of Moses. Moses wrote these as the words "which the Lord had commanded to Israel" (8:1).

7. Read 2 Timothy 3:16, 17. How much of the Bible did God inspire?

8. How might a Christian show that he believes the Bible is God's Word?

Because he highly regarded God's Word, Nehemiah supported the people's request to hear Ezra read it. Nehemiah clearly did not feel threatened by Ezra. If anything, he graciously deferred to him. Nehemiah felt at home in the role God had assigned to him and was pleased to respect the role God had assigned to Ezra.

As a descendent of Aaron's third son, Ezra legitimately held the office of "priest" (8:2; cf. Ezra 7:1–5). As a priest, Ezra represented the people to God in acts of sacred worship in the temple. When Ezra returned to Jerusalem in 458 BC, his central purpose was to introduce spiritual revival and reform by faithfully and carefully proclaiming the Word of God. He had actually been commissioned by Artaxerxes to teach the Scriptures upon his return (cf. Ezra 7:25, 26). Nehemiah wisely recognized Ezra's gifts and office and utilized his skills.

Ezra placed a great stress on the people's "understanding" (8:2; cf. 3, 7, 8, 12, 13). This revival was not driven primarily by emotions—but by the clear teaching of God's revealed Word, accompanied by an obedient response.

9. What often happens to a person's decision when it is based on a strong emotional appeal?

10. Think back to the important spiritual decisions you have made. What part did emotion and what part did God's Word play in making your decision a lasting decision?

## Nehemiah Listened to God's Word

In willing response to the request of the people, Ezra boldly read the law (8:3, 5, 8). Nehemiah carefully listened with the rest of the congregation.

11. Why is a leader not exempt from needing to hear God's Word preached?

12. What could a church do in order to give their pastor an opportunity to sit under someone else's preaching on occasion?

Ezra read aloud from the scroll "from the morning until midday" (8:3a). As he read, the men, women, and children listened attentively (8:3b). Some scholars suggest that as many as 30,000 to 50,000 gathered to hear these words. In such a crowd, it would be difficult to see Ezra as he read. For this reason, the tall "pulpit" (platform) had been constructed (8:4).

When Ezra took the scroll and began to open it, the crowd immediately stood to its feet (8:5). Apparently they were standing for this entire time—demonstrating their dedication, reverence and readiness to hear. Most of these people would not have had personal copies of the scrolls of the Hebrew Bible, so even hearing it in this way would have been a very special experience.

13. How would you respond if your pastor asked you to stand while he preached for several hours?

Displaying a spirit of adoration and worship to God, Ezra proclaimed, "Bless the Lord!" All the people answered in unison, "Amen! Amen," lifted their hands, "bowed their heads, and worshipped the Lord with their faces to the ground" (8:6). The message immediately produced repentance in the people, some of whom doubtless had never heard the message of Scripture before in such an elaborate context.

After a spirit of worship had been established, Ezra read the words of the law clearly and understandably. Moses' writings would have been very difficult for them, as his books were now 1,000 years old. Doubtless Aramaic was still the first language for many of the Jews, thus Ezra must have translated the Hebrew text.

It is fruitless to hear the Word of God without understanding what it means. Proper interpretation is vital to Bible study and teaching. Ezra and his associates demonstrated both, first observing what the text said, then explaining what the text meant (8:7, 8). The process of handling the Word of God remains the same in this New Testament age. It is only after these steps have been followed that proper applications of the text can be made.

14. Read 1 Corinthians 2:12–14. What help in understanding the Bible does a believer have according to this verse?

## Nehemiah Challenged the People to Respond

Even the correct interpretation of God's Word—although essential—is not ultimately enough. The Word must be received with the correct attitude and then put into action. Four basic questions help us put Scripture into action: What does it say? What does it mean? How should I respond? What should I do? These questions become four basic steps in authentic Bible-learning.

15. How faithful are you at completing the four basic steps in authentic Bible-learning?

16. What will a person take away from the Scriptures if his practice is to read them until something strikes him as interesting?




While Nehemiah was neither a scribe nor a priest, he recognized the influence his position had among the people, and he wanted to use this influence for their spiritual well-being. Because the Feast of Trumpets (civil New Year) had arrived and Nehemiah was Jerusalem's civil leader, it was appropriate for him to address the assembly. In a stirring but brief speech, Nehemiah challenged the people to stop their crying (8:9) and respond with joy to God's Word (8:10).

Ezra's proclamation of the law had a powerful impact. Perhaps the magnitude of the captivity's significance was just now becoming apparent to some of the Jewish people. The gravity of their national disobedience struck them.

While Nehemiah was no doubt pleased with their sensitivity to the Lord and His Word, he did not want the people to fall into morbid introspection. God's will for Israel on the Feast of Trumpets was to rejoice in Him! Nehemiah was calling for the appropriate response. The Scriptural significance of the day was to triumph over the people's immediate emotional reaction to what they were learning.

"The joy of the LORD is your strength," he exclaimed (8:10). He also told the people to go and eat the feast of celebration, and to give ample food to those who were less fortunate. Everyone, then, could celebrate the feast with joy. Their introspection was to turn to fellowship and sharing in acts of kindness to others.

17. How much spiritual growth will a believer have if he concentrates only on how far short he falls of God's standard for his life?

The Levites supported what Nehemiah told the assembly and the people took the counsel to heart (8:11, 12). They celebrated the Lord's goodness and provided food and drink to those in need. God's Word made a tremendous impression on Jerusalem. With the help of Ezra, the Levites and Nehemiah, the people experienced the full cycle of spiritual learning. While it can be said that the city was revived by the rebuilding of the walls, it might also be said that the people were revived by the proclamation of the Word.

## The People Demonstrated Willingness to Obey

The next day, the head of every household met with Ezra and the Levites to hear more of God's Word (8:13). As they listened, they learned about the Feast of Booths and the command to celebrate this feast as well (8:14). The feast commemorated God's provision for the people when He brought them out of Egypt and cared for them in the wilderness even when they had no place to dwell. It also looks ahead to the time when God will dwell with His people directly in the Millennial Kingdom.

The people had two weeks to prepare for the celebration. According to the laws of celebration, the people were to make "booths" or shelters to use for this celebration.

Once again, responding to God's Word willingly, the people went into nearby woods and brought back what they need to construct the booths (8:15, 16).

This Feast of Booths made all the people of Judah glad (8:17)—especially since they had not celebrated this feast as a unified nation since the days of Joshua. This celebration gave Jerusalem the new spiritual start it so desperately needed.

18. Why does reading God's Word and obeying it make us glad?


On the final day, the celebration concluded with "a solemn assembly." The people added this "eighth day" to the Feast of Tabernacles

(8:18), apparently based on Deuteronomy 31:9–13, which calls for a time every seventh year at this feast when the priests were to read the entire law of God to the people. Since it would have been many decades, at minimum, since this was done, the people elected to have it done at this crucial time.

God's Word brought spiritual renewal to Jerusalem. Today, too, spiritual renewal results from rekindled devotion to Scripture. When God's people revere and obey the Bible, righteousness pervades their lives and impacts society.

### Making It Personal

19. What is the best time of the day for you to read and study the Bible?

20. Should you be giving the Bible more attention in your own personal life and has this lesson caused you to think of that?

21. Perhaps, like these Jews, you should set aside some special extended time, even if a holiday or a vacation is not imminent, to reconnect with God through His Word. When will you seek to set aside time to seek God in His Word?

22. Memorize Ephesians 5:15–17.

# Set the Example!

*A spiritual leader sets the right example.*

## Nehemiah 9:1–38

**"Brethren, be followers together of me, and mark them which walk so as ye have us for an ensample" (Philippians 3:17).**

Someone once said, "Remember, people will judge you by your actions, not your intentions. You may have a heart of gold—but so does a hard-boiled egg." And Edmund Burke, an eighteenth century philosopher, said, "Example is the school of mankind, and they will learn at no other."

There is no escaping the truth of those statements. The examples of our lives speak louder than the instructions of our lips.

## Getting Started

1. Name three people who are following your example, whether you realize it or not.


2. Do those who follow you learn more from what you teach or how you live? Explain.

The testimony of our lives is much louder than the lessons from our lips. Nehemiah knew that principle well. He was a leader who taught godliness with his life.

## Searching the Scriptures

God's people normally respond well to godly spiritual leadership. And Nehemiah had won the strong admiration of the people. This chapter unfolds five behaviors of Nehemiah that the people copied.

### The People Fasted—As Nehemiah Had

The chapter begins just two days after the conclusion of the extended Feast of Tabernacles that the nation had observed in Nehemiah 8, and roughly a month after the completion of the wall project (cf. 6:15).

It seems ironic that the people observed a period of fasting so soon after a period of feasting. This is especially true since Nehemiah himself had asked the people to rejoice instead of weep (see 8:9, 10). Perhaps the timing is better understood in light of the "solemn assembly" that ended the Feast of Booths (Neh. 8:18). Just as the 40 years in the wilderness climaxed with the awesome responsibility to conquer the land, this Feast of Booths would climax with the awesome responsibility to be wise stewards of the land freshly repossessed.

A whole day transpired between the solemn meeting and the opening events of chapter 9. It was now Tishri 24. The meeting had closed the feast on Tishri 22. Those who lingered had chosen to do so. This period of fasting was not required by the law. Why then did these people fast?

The Jerusalemites had more than likely acquired the practice of fasting from their spiritual leader, Nehemiah (cf. Neh. 1:4). Upon first hearing of the devastation in Jerusalem from Hanani, Nehemiah set aside his own physical needs and desires and committed himself totally to this concern.

3. How might a leader show his commitment to the Lord today?

4. Is fasting an appropriate way for a leader to show his commitment to God? Explain.

5. Read Matthew 6:16–18. What instructions did Jesus give concerning fasting?

## The People Mourned—As Nehemiah Had

The people wore sackcloth and humbly placed "earth upon them" when they fasted (9:1b). Once again, they followed the pattern Nehemiah had set (cf. Neh. 1:4).

But why would the people mourn? They had rebuilt Jerusalem's walls, and they had just experienced revival. Even Nehemiah had recently proclaimed, "The joy of the LORD is your strength" (8:10).

The context explains why the people of Jerusalem mourned. Judah had indeed been restored, but it was not yet free (see 9:37). Judah was still a province of Persia. It still owed taxes and loyalty to the king. The people had Persia's favor now, but would they have it tomorrow? Such favor wasn't guaranteed by any means! The people would later say, "We are in great distress" (9:37b).

As Nehemiah had lamented before the Lord, so the people brought their concern before God.

6. Read 1 Peter 5:7. What does this verse ask believers to do?

7. How does a leader affect those he leads when he publically casts his cares on the Lord?

## The People Confessed—As Nehemiah Had

When Nehemiah had first heard the news of Judah's plight, he confessed his sins and Judah's sins before the Lord (1:6b, 7). Nehemiah did so because he knew that sin had led to Jerusalem's chastisement. Now that the people realized they were still under Persian rule (Neh. 9), they must have perceived this "bondage" as chastisement for their sin. This discipline was in accordance with what God had predicted in Deuteronomy 28—30.

For this reason, they separated themselves from all the non-Jews in the city, and listened intently to the reading of the law for three hours (Neh. 9:2, 3). For the three hours after that, they confessed their sins before the Lord.

8. Does a leader help his people by pretending to be perfect and never needing to confess his sins? Explain.

9. What cautions might a leader use when confessing his sins before others?

This separation "from all strangers" (9:2) appears to involve divorce from non-Jewish wives. In Ezra 10, similar action was taken by means of a detailed ceremony that included "a covenant with our God to put away all the wives, and such as are born of them, ...according to the law" (Ezra 10:3).

Even as Nehemiah had confessed the sins of the people of Judah from whom he was far removed by distance, so the people confessed the sins of their ancestors from whom they were far removed by time. They also realized, however, that they were guilty of having the same attitudes.

## The People Worshiped—As Nehemiah Had

Worship had become customary to Nehemiah. He repeated the

worshipful title, "God of heaven," numerous times in his book. He also took a strong role in leading the people in worship during the Feast of Trumpets and the Feast of Booths (chapter 8). It is not surprising, then, that the congregation of Jerusalem turned to God in spontaneous worship (9:3).

10. Describe the worship of a leader who is mostly interested in drawing attention to himself instead of God?

11. Why is worship something we can't convincingly pretend to do?

The prayer that followed the Bible reading and the confession of sins resembles the pattern of a descriptive praise psalm, as the people praised the Lord for Who He is and for what He had done.

## The People Prayed—As Nehemiah Had

Most of the verses in Nehemiah 9 report the prayer of the people (vv. 5–38) in confessing their sins and in worshiping the Lord. Reading through the book of Nehemiah, we learn to appreciate the frequency with which Nehemiah himself prayed. This man of prayer had influenced the people of Jerusalem to be people of prayer.

In Nehemiah 1:4–11, Nehemiah prayed for favor with the king. God answered that prayer with an opportunity to present his distress and Jerusalem's dilemma. Secondly, Nehemiah uttered a brief and silent prayer for wisdom while addressing the king (2:4). God granted Nehemiah wisdom, and the result was the king's blessing and decree to rebuild. During days of ridicule, Nehemiah prayed (4:1–5), and God caused the work to continue. In 4:9, Nehemiah prayed concerning his enemies, and in answer to that prayer their plan was thwarted. Nehemiah also prayed during Jerusalem's internal conflict (5:19), and God guided the people through Nehemiah into a state of determination. Nehemiah later prayed for strength to hold up during the wicked plots against his life, and God gave him strength (6:9). In that same context Nehemiah asked God for protection, and God gave His blessing and protection (6:14).

The people made their prayer to the eternal, all-powerful God of creation. Since He is unique and set apart, and knows His people best, He is able to solve the issues that trouble them. As these men rehearsed the history of Israel in prayer, they first made it clear that they understood the importance of giving glory to the Lord as their creator.

12. Read Nehemiah 9:5, 6. Why is recognizing God as the creator a good place to start a worshipful prayer to God?

13. Read Nehemiah 9:7–30. Record some of the attributes of God that are obvious from His relationship with Israel throughout their history.

14. How can a leader draw attention to those same attributes?

As the leaders move into the body of their prayer, they retrace the history of Israel, beginning with the call of Abraham and the unconditional covenant that God gave to him (9:7, 8).

They then moved on to discuss the Exodus, a summary of the revelation of the Mosaic Law given at Mount Sinai, and the provision from God during their wilderness wanderings (9:9–15).

Then those praying explain the failure of Israel—unbelief (9:16, 17). Even here, they are quick to mention that Lord is "a God ready to pardon, gracious and merciful, slow to anger, and of great kindness" (9:17). Although the people had failed terribly at the incident of the golden calf, God did not forsake them (9:18, 19). Instead of giving the nation what it deserved, God directed and blessed Israel and gave them the chosen land (9:22–25).

These external blessings, however, were not sufficient to produce righteousness in God's people. They cast God's "law behind their backs" (9:26) and killed God's prophets. Such disobedience led to God's chastening (9:27). Even though God showed mercy, this cycle kept repeating (9:28–30).

God was faithful to His covenants with Israel, and His never-failing mercy kept Him from consuming them (9:31). The people recognized these truths and freely admitted their guilt before their faithful God (9:33–35). They encouraged themselves by remembering God's marvelous dealings with them all throughout the history of the nation, while also praying for new and fresh mercies from Him to meet their current challenges.

15. What blessing has God given to you that are worth remembering as you worship Him?



16. What part should remembering God's grace and mercy play in a leader's public prayer?



By the end of the prayer, we realize that the nation had come full circle—they were back in the Promised Land, but as "servants" of the Persian king, who was reaping the benefits of the land and their hard labors (9:36, 37). The people summed up their situation by stating, "We are in great distress" (9:37).

The people were in need of salvation from their enemies, such as they had experienced at the time of the Exodus. Nehemiah, like Moses, was uniquely qualified to lead the people at this time since he had left a place of prominence in a foreign government. Anyone in the land who had spiritual discernment must have been exceedingly grateful to have the privilege of being associated with this God-ordained leader, and we can certainly infer that he appreciated their prayers as well.

## The People Remembered—As Nehemiah Had

When Nehemiah prayed at the beginning of his book, he based his request on God's covenant (Neh. 1:5–11). It is striking to note that in the people's prayer, they, too, prayed to the "God, who keepest covenant" (9:32). Notice also the similarity of 9:32 to Nehemiah's statement in 4:14. Evidently his emphasis had made an impact on those who had learned from his example. Nehemiah's theological concept of God took root in the people's hearts.

God made a covenant with Abraham in Genesis 12:1–3. He promised to give Abraham a land, a special offspring, and a world-wide blessing. This covenant was unconditional, literal, and eternal. It was reaffirmed to Moses in the Palestinian (Land) Covenant (Deut. 30), reaffirmed to David in the Davidic Covenant (2 Sam. 7), and reaffirmed to Jeremiah in the New Covenant (Jer. 32). The side of the covenant known as the Mosaic Covenant promised the people blessing if they obeyed the Lord and chastisement if they disobeyed (Exod. 20).

As chapter 9 of Nehemiah concludes, the people of Jerusalem made a covenant with God—to do all that He commanded them. Their covenant was based upon His covenant (9:38).

Like the children of Issachar almost 600 years earlier, whom Ezra wrote about, these people "had understanding of the times, to know what Israel ought to do" (1 Chron. 12:32). Such knowledge was based in a deep comprehension of Biblical history. Notice that their lengthy prayer focused on the great truths about God, His work among His people, and the overwhelming needs of the nation in light of its current situation. Noticeably absent from their petitions is a focus on the subjective, personal preferences of these people. While those things are not unimportant, they were put in proper perspective by all that the people had learned from Ezra's teaching in chapter 8.

## Making It Personal

17. Which of Nehemiah's actions are not prevalent in your life?

18. What do you need to do to become a better example in those areas?

19. Identify two people you want to influence toward godliness.

20. What will you do to enhance your godly influence on their lives?

21. Memorize Philippians 3:17.

# Trust and Obey

*A spiritual leader stimulates others to trust and obey God.*

## Nehemiah 10; 11

**"Who is among you that feareth the LORD, that obeyeth the voice of his servant, that walketh in darkness, and hath no light? let him trust in the name of the LORD, and stay upon his God" (Isaiah 50:10).**

Take a minute and say the pledge to your country's flag. Now say it again, but this time think about the pledge you are making. Let the words resonate in your mind.

Stopping to think about the words should give you a fresh understanding of the pledge.

Too often as believers we "pledge" our lives to God with about the same seriousness we have as we pledge ourselves to our country. God deserves our full, serious attention as we live for Him.

## Getting Started

1. How serious are you when you normally say the pledge to your country's flag?

2. What difference does saying the pledge make in your life?



Our ultimate allegiance should be to God. We ought to trust Him and therefore seriously pledge to obey Him. This lesson provides an example of a pledge to God.

## Searching the Scriptures

After God brought revival to Jerusalem's population through the public reading of the Scriptures (Neh. 8), the people conducted a spontaneous six-hour public prayer meeting (9:3). Such a meeting had not occurred since the dedication of Solomon's temple (2 Chron. 6:12–42). At the conclusion of Jerusalem's heartfelt prayer, the people made a new commitment before the Lord (Neh. 9:38). Nehemiah chapter 10 gives the details of that public commitment.

### Makers of the Oath

In the first section of chapter 10, Nehemiah records the names of all who signed this binding agreement with the Lord. Exercising his leadership, Nehemiah was the first to sign (10:1). By signing this contract, he identified with the people of Jerusalem and publicly pledged his dependence upon God and his obedience to Him.

Following Nehemiah's lead, the other civil leaders and religious leaders put their seals to the agreement. Twenty-four princes and priests (10:1–8), seventeen Levites (10:9–13), and forty-four heads of families (10:14–27) signed the agreement. Since it was impossible for everyone to sign the document, the rest of the people aligned with these leaders by making a verbal oath (10:28, 29).

This was a very serious obligation that the people were entering into. Ecclesiastes 5:1–7 makes this concept quite clear: "Better is it that thou shouldest not vow, than that thou shouldest vow and not pay" (Eccl. 5:5). Jephthah probably provided the greatest example in the Bible of a foolish vow (cf. Judges 11:30–40).

While the vow the Jews made was not foolish, it was very serious, and the people bound themselves "and entered into a curse, and into an oath, to walk in God's law, which was given by Moses the servant of God, and to observe and do all the commandments of the LORD our Lord, and his judgments and his statutes" (Neh. 10:29).

Such open, public commitments were related to the fact that the Old Testament people of God were a nation living together in covenant with Him. They were, in essence, committing to obey that which was already binding upon them.

In the New Testament, the emphasis is not on making such public types of vows, but rather on making sure that we always abide by the commitments we make through our words in the course of all kinds of conversation. Jesus emphasized this in Matthew 5:33–37, and James reiterated this concept in James 5:12.

3. Read James 5:12 and summarize the principle of this verse.

The Apostle Peter attempted to make grandiose claims on occasion (cf. Matt. 26:35; Mark 14:31; Luke 22:33), but learned through experience that these statements were easier to make than to keep, and far less important than obedience without presumption (cf. Luke 22:34; 54–62).

## Terms of the Oath

The bottom line of the pledge that the people in Nehemiah's time made to God is recorded in Nehemiah 10:29. Jerusalem's citizens promised "to observe and do all the commandments of the Lord our Lord, and his judgments and his statutes." Here, again, the three aspects of the law of Moses are referred to. In this oath, the people promised to keep all of God's moral, civil, and ceremonial laws. In both Nehemiah's prayer (1:7) and the people's prayer (9:34), those praying confessed that they violated all three aspects of God's law.

As the people came off of their experiences in chapters 8 and 9, the types of sins that had brought the Babylonian Captivity on the nation were foremost on their minds. Thus, they made this pledge that dealt with the basic areas of marriage (10:30), the observation of the Sabbath Day and Sabbatical Year (10:31), the care of the house of God, and the matters of offerings and the giving of firstfruits and tithes (10:32–39).

In taking this solemn oath, the people actually pledged themselves to their own curse (Neh. 10:29). They invited God's chastisement if they would fail to obey.

God had specifically commanded the people of Israel not to inter-marry with those who were not the covenant people (Exod. 34:14–16). He did so to preserve their spiritual purity, not as a matter of racism. Such intermarriage, however, became a besetting sin of Israel. They fell into this sin as soon as they occupied the Promised Land, and God had to judge them (Judges 3:5–8). During the period of monarchy, Solomon led the nation into chaos and schism as a result of his blatant disobedi-ence in this regard (1 Kings 10—12). Even when the people returned to Jerusalem from captivity, they brought this sin with them (Ezra 9; 10). And we have already seen the disastrous results of this type of behavior here in the book of Nehemiah (6:17–19). The prophet Malachi had also come to preach against sins of this type (cf. Mal. 2:13–17).

The nation never seemed to learn. But now, they made a specific promise to God that this would never happen again.

4. Why would it have been tempting for the Jews to intermarry with pagans as they returned from captivity?




5. Read 1 Corinthians 6:14—7:1. What did Paul say concerning in-termarrying with unbelievers?




6. What might make this a difficult command for believers to obey today?

The people promised to be a testimony for God in the marketplace (Neh. 10:31). In the law, God had commanded the people of Israel to keep the Sabbath day holy as a day of rest (Exod. 20:8–11). Motivated by greed and selfish ambition, the people had frequently violated this law. They valued material gain over their identification with the Lord of the Sabbath. They now pledged to observe the Sabbath just as God required.

After all, it had been due in part to her violation of the law of the seventh-year Sabbath (cf. Lev. 25:1–7) that Judah had suffered the Babylonian/Medo-Persian captivity. God had warned that there would be one year of captivity for every year of failure to institute this law (cf. 2 Chron. 36:20, 21).

7. God does not now require believers to keep the Sabbath, but how might greed and selfish ambition show themselves in a believer's life today?

In the final specific pledge of the agreement, the people promised to support God's work financially (Neh. 10:32–39). They promised to give the temple an annual offering of a third of a shekel (10:32). Although financial aid had been received from the Persian Empire (under Cyrus, Darius, and Artaxerxes), this subsidy was soon to expire. Furthermore, God's law required an annual offering of half a shekel (cf. Exod. 30:11–16), so this accommodation was a sign of their poverty.

Offerings received at the temple provided for the showbread, sacrifices, feasts, and other services (Neh. 10:33). The Lord's work depended on the faithful giving of God's people.

Other promises included the contribution of wood to burn on the altar of sacrifice (cf. Lev. 6:12, 13), the bringing of the firstfruits of crops and trees (cf. Exod. 23:19), and the dedication of their firstborn sons and animals (Exod. 22:29; Deut. 12:6).

8. What is the correlation between a person's faith in God and his giving?

The final words of this oath appear in Nehemiah 10:39 and sum up all that the people had covenanted to do together: "We will not forsake the house of our God."

Would the people be able to follow through on these wonderful, eloquent words of promise and hope? The answer will come before the end of the book.

9. What does dedication to God mean for us as church age believers who are not under the law but under grace?

## An Act of Trust

Obedience and trust work hand-in-hand. Having entered into a covenant of spiritual renewal with their Lord, the people were now ready to repopulate the city of Jerusalem confidently. Now that they were living in obedience to God's laws, they did not need to fear His chastisement in the form of either a military attack or bondage.

Although Nehemiah had laid the groundwork for the city's resettlement in chapter 7, he had known the timing was not yet right and the work was not complete. (He learned to become sensitive to timing during these years of walking with the Lord.) In light of the spiritual happenings recorded through chapters 8, 9, and 10, the people were now ready for the next phase of Nehemiah's plan.

## Settlement in Jerusalem

The rulers who dwelt at Jerusalem (11:1) were there primarily to maintain the temple.

By casting lots, the leaders determined who else should be included in the ten percent of Judah's population to relocate inside the rebuilt holy city (11:1).

The use of lots prevented favoritism or inequity in such a serious choice. All those who were selected no doubt accepted this as God's sovereign will, for they moved to Jerusalem willingly (11:2).

All totaled, 3,044 men (and their families) moved from the general region of Judah to inside the city walls of Jerusalem. These included 468 from the tribe of Judah, 928 from the tribe of Benjamin, 1,192 priests, 284 Levites, and 172 porters (or gatekeepers). Nehemiah's careful plan had now been implemented.

## Settlement near Jerusalem

Others of the tribe of Judah settled in 17 towns and communities near Jerusalem (11:25–30). Some settled as far south as Beersheba, 32 miles away.

North of Judah, some of the tribe of Benjamin settled in 15 towns and villages (11:31–35). The remaining Levites settled in both regions (11:36). Nehemiah certainly exercised grace along with his regulatory plan.

Everything appeared to be in perfect order within the rebuilt city, but there were still sinful, fallen people living inside those walls, as well as in all the other cities in Judah.

10. When have you failed to keep a promise you made to God?

11. To what did you attribute your failure?

12. Why can't we count on our good intentions as the impetus for spiritual growth in our lives?

13. What can we count on to help us grow spiritually?

The promises that these people made would only be as good as their ability to keep them under pressure.

## Making It Personal

14. In what ways do you need to grow spiritually?

15. What steps will you take to facilitate growth in those areas of your life?

Remember that spiritual growth will not take place outside of God's grace. Your promise to grow will not automatically translate into actual growth. As you put your faith in God and seek Him through His Word and prayer, He will empower you through His Spirit to grow.

16. Commit in your own heart to especially seek God's help to overcome any besetting sins (Heb. 12:1).

17. Memorize Isaiah 50:10.

# Compromising Again

*A spiritual leader guides others into dedication and separation to God.*

## Nehemiah 12; 13

**"Blessed is the man that walketh not in the counsel of the ungodly, nor standeth in the way of sinners, nor sitteth in the seat of the scornful. But his delight is in the law of the LORD; and in his law doth he meditate day and night"** **(Psalm 1:1, 2).**

The United States government has a food pyramid that provides a guide for us as we choose which foods to eat. Most people don't pay any attention to that food pyramid. Most people, however, do pay attention to TV ads for food products. That could be a problem for some. If a person ate foods according to how frequently they were advertised, he would end up flipping that food pyramid on its head—eating just a small amount of healthy foods and a large amount of unhealthy foods. Anyone on a weight-loss diet would be tempted to compromise his diet every time he watched TV.

## Getting Started

1. If you were on a diet, what food would tempt you the most to compromise your diet?

2. What special steps might you take to keep from eating that food?


Nehemiah celebrated the dedication of the wall of Jerusalem with the Jews before he went back to visit the king of Persia. When he returned from Persia he found that many of the Jews had compromised and given in to the ungodly influences of the people who lived around them. He then dealt with their sin as a wise leader.

## Searching the Scriptures

For the people of Jerusalem to build 2.6 miles of city wall in a period of 52 days was a monumental accomplishment in the strength and grace of God (Neh. 6:16). This called for a spectacular celebration. Having just gone through a purging process of spiritual revival, the people wanted this to be a God-honoring celebration as well. Unfortunately, this is not the end of the story. After Nehemiah went back to Persia and later returned to Judah, he discovered that the people were back to their old sins. He therefore concluded his ministry with an urgent appeal for separation from evil.

### Dedication of the Walls

As a good leader, Nehemiah honored faithful servants of the Lord by giving the names of those serving in the temple (Neh. 12). First, he listed the post-exilic temple leaders. His recognition of these men reveals his understanding of Jerusalem. The wall of Jerusalem received its importance because of what it protected—God's holy temple! He included the leaders of the priests (vv. 1–7), the priests' helpers (vv. 8, 9), the high priests (vv. 10, 11), the heads of the priestly families (vv. 12–21), and other Levites and priestly associates (vv. 22–26).

Nehemiah 12:27–47 continues the historical narrative from 11:2. Although the walls had been finished for some time (see Nehemiah 6:15), dedication ceremonies were not held until Jerusalem was successfully reestablished. At this stage Nehemiah could also celebrate the completion of his task. As the dedication ceremonies were planned, emphasis was placed on the service as a rendering of "thanks" to God (12:31).

The purpose of the celebration is given in 12:27. Levites were enlisted to provide music of "gladness" (12:27–29). Both vocalists and instrumentalists were summoned to provide songs of thanksgiving and praise.

Before the actual dedication could begin, both the wall and the worshipers had to be ceremonially clean (12:30). Priests, Levites, and the general Jewish public were all cleansed. Nehemiah seems to indicate that the blood of animal sacrifices was sprinkled on the walls and gates.

3. Read Nehemiah 12:30. Why was it important to dedicate the people before dedicating the wall?

4. What implications does this have for today as we seek to do the Lord's work?

Nehemiah took a major role in planning this spectacular dedication. He appointed two choirs of thanksgiving to encircle the city on top of the walls. Both choirs were evidently to start at the Valley Gate.

Ezra led one of these choirs. This choir included Hoshaiah, half of the leaders, and priests with trumpets and other instrumentalists. At the signal, this group marched counterclockwise around the city on top of the wall (12:31–37).

The other group included Nehemiah, half of the officials, priests with trumpets, and other singers. This group marched clockwise around the city on the wall at the same time (12:38–42).

What an experience of worship and celebration this must have created. It not only directed Jerusalem's praise to God for the new wall, but it also gave a powerful testimony to all the onlookers surrounding the city. Perhaps even Tobiah was watching.

5. Read Nehemiah 4:3. What did Tobiah say about the wall as the Jews were building it?

6. How do you think he reacted to large groups of Jews walking on the wall?

These two choirs evidently met inside the city walls, because they completed their elaborate dedication ceremony at the temple with the offering of many sacrifices.

The author summarizes: "That day they offered great sacrifices, and rejoiced: for God had made them rejoice with great joy" (12:43).

7. What connection do you see between the completed walls and the great joy the people had?

8. When have you seen the connection between obedience to God and great joy in your life?

9. What happens to our level of joy when we try to avoid serving God, particularly service that requires serious dedication?

At the conclusion of the service, Nehemiah directed the people in the giving of contributions, firstfruits, and tithes, just as they had promised to do in the oath recorded in chapter 10. Temple workers received what they needed, and all the holy vessels were "sanctified." With the completion of the wall and the reconstructing of Jerusalem, the temple of God also got a fresh start.

## Separation of the People

Nehemiah's first term as governor had been most successful. During the twelve years of that term (445–433 BC; Neh. 5:14), he had rebuilt a strong civil and moral foundation for Judah's future. His long tenure had demonstrated a genuine commitment to Jerusalem's welfare, and not just a passing interest. However, he finally returned to Persia (cf. 2:6; 13:6).

In Nehemiah's absence, the people of Jerusalem quickly lapsed into their old sinful ways. During those years of Nehemiah's absence, however, the prophet Malachi confronted the people with their backsliding (Mal. 1:6—3:12).

10. Read Malachi 1:6–14; 2:17; and 3:1–5. How does Malachi characterize the Jews' service for God?

11. What was the Jews' basic problem (see 3:5)?

12. Have you had times in your life when you just went through the motions of serving God without actually reverencing Him?

Nehemiah was shocked when he returned to Judah for his second term as the governor-in-chief (Neh. 13:7, 8).

## Separation from Pagans

Nehemiah discovered a flagrant violation of the laws of Moses. Jews were inviting Ammonites and Moabites to worship at the holy temple! Historically, these tribes had tried to bar the children of Israel from possessing the land of promise (see Deut. 23:3–6). They even tried to curse Israel with the help of the false prophet Balaam (Num. 22—25). Nehemiah boldly had these portions of the law read to the people once again, and immediately they took action and corrected the matter (Neh. 13:1–3).

## Separation from Compromise

Nehemiah further discovered in horror that the high priest Eliashib had invited Tobiah, the enemy of Jerusalem, to live in the temple. Eliashib helped Tobiah set up housekeeping in one of the storerooms (13:4, 5).

Nehemiah became furious when he saw what had happened. He knew from personal experience that Tobiah was not only an Ammonite, but he was also an enemy of Jerusalem and of the true God. Now Tobiah could oppose the work of God from within!

13. What message would Eliashib have sent to the Jews when he made such arrangements for Tobiah?


Nehemiah must have been deeply puzzled at Eliashib's compromise. Perhaps 13:4 gives the explanation. Tobiah and Eliashib may have been related to each other. If so, here is more evidence that pagan intermarriage produces tragic consequences.

According to Nehemiah 13:8 and 9, Nehemiah took immediate action. He stormed the storeroom and threw out all of Tobiah's "household stuff." This was followed by immediate ceremonial cleansing and the return of the room to temple service.

## Separation from Worldly Materialism

One reason Tobiah could live in a temple storeroom was that many of these storerooms were empty (13:5). People had stopped giving to the work of God. Temple supplies had run low, and many Levites and temple servants had to work elsewhere to avoid starving (13:10).

Thus, the ongoing sin of financial neglect was compounded by the neglecting of the temple servants (13:10). Furthermore, with the Levites absent from their temple service, the temple programs most likely suffered.

How quickly the people of Jerusalem forgot their oath, "We will not forsake the house of our God" (Neh. 10:39). They distinctly violated every area of the promises they had made in Nehemiah 10:29–39.

Again, Malachi rebuked the people sharply for their lack of giving during this period of time (cf. Mal. 3:8–12).

14. Read Malachi 3:8–12. What point did God make about Himself in these verses through His prophet Malachi?

15. What should you think about the notion that a believer could gain something of greater value by being disobedient to God?

This situation called for rededication and for accountability to God's law through His appointed leaders. Nehemiah immediately appointed four temple leaders to oversee the giving of tithes and offerings. And again, he prayed (Neh.13:13, 14).

Jerusalem's population was also more concerned about making money than keeping the Sabbath. As Nehemiah walked around the town one Sabbath, he saw Jews buying and selling and transporting the merchandise of craftsmen (13:15–18). All the markets were open and busy.

Nehemiah probably remembered the oath the people had taken to keep the Sabbath (10:31). He immediately provided a remedy as governor.

16. Read Nehemiah 13:17–22. How would you describe the actions Nehemiah took in dealing with the Sabbath violators? Was he being a wise leader?

First, Nehemiah confronted the people for profaning the Sabbath (13:17). He reminded them that this activity was the very cause for which God brought the captivity on Judah (13:18). Second, he ordered that all the city gates be kept shut on the Sabbath (Neh. 13:19). Third, he appointed guards to see to it that no hucksters came near the city. Finally, Nehemiah threatened to personally throw any huckster away from the city walls who failed to comply with these regulations (13:20, 21).

## Separation from Godless Intermarriage

The last paragraph of Nehemiah's book reveals that this brokenhearted spiritual leader had to deal again with Israel's besetting sin—intermarriage with pagans. Remembering their oath not to intermarry (10:30), and that they swore to their own curse, Nehemiah held them to it by calling down these curses on them (13:25).

17. Read Nehemiah 13:25–28. What did Nehemiah do to deal with the Jews' intermarriage with pagans?

18. What do his actions say about the seriousness of the sin?

After cleansing the priesthood and reappointing the temple leaders to their rightful tasks, Nehemiah closed his book in a manner so characteristic of this great man—he prayed (13:31). He can rightly be called a "spiritual man" and a "leader."

These short prayers in the midst of busy days were one of the hallmarks of Nehemiah's great spiritual leadership. It was such prayers, mixed into the midst of much hard labor, that gave Nehemiah the power to accomplish all that he did in the face of such a desperate situation.

## Making It Personal

19. Why do we compromise and grasp for what we shouldn't have as believers?

20. Have you compromised and followed after particular sins? If so, deal with them with the same seriousness Nehemiah had in dealing with them.

The book of Nehemiah began with Nehemiah's brokenness as God's chosen leader to rebuild Jerusalem. His brokenness paved the way for the building of the walls and the restoration of the Jews.

Our spiritual growth begins with brokenness too. If we are living away from God, He wants us to respond first by confessing our sins. He then will start the building process in our lives and will be able to make us into the type of leader He wants us to be.

21. Memorize Psalm 1:1 and 2.